THE
GREAT
GOULD

THE GREAT GOULD

PETER GODDARD

DUNDURN
TORONTO

Printer: Friesens

Library and Archives Canada Cataloguing in Publication

Goddard, Peter, author
    The Great Gould / Peter Goddard.

Issued in print and electronic formats.
ISBN 978-1-4597-3309-1 (hardcover).--ISBN 978-1-4597-3310-7 (PDF).--
ISBN 978-1-4597-3311-4 (EPUB)

    1. Gould, Glenn, 1932-1982. 2. Pianists--Canada--Biography.
I. Title.

ML417.G69G57 2017   786.2092   C2017-901846-9
                                        C2017-901847-7

1 2 3 4 5   21 20 19 18 17

We acknowledge the support of the **Canada Council for the Arts**, which last year invested $153 million to bring the arts to Canadians throughout the country, and the **Ontario Arts Council** for our publishing program. We also acknowledge the financial support of the **Government of Ontario**, through the **Ontario Book Publishing Tax Credit** and the **Ontario Media Development Corporation**, and the **Government of Canada**.

Nous remercions le **Conseil des arts du Canada** de son soutien. L'an dernier, le Conseil a investi 153 millions de dollars pour mettre de l'art dans la vie des Canadiennes et des Canadiens de tout le pays.

Care has been taken to trace the ownership of copyright material used in this book. The author and the publisher welcome any information enabling them to rectify any references or credits in subsequent editions.
        — *J. Kirk Howard, President*

The publisher is not responsible for websites or their content unless they are owned by the publisher.

Printed and bound in Canada.

VISIT US AT

  dundurn.com | @dundurnpress | dundurnpress | dundurnpress

Dundurn
3 Church Street, Suite 500
Toronto, Ontario, Canada
M5E 1M2

Baby Gould pondering his fingers.

To Carol Ann

CONTENTS

He also spelled his name with three *n*'s.

INTRODUCTION

As a kid doing my daily piano practice in a suburban basement west of Toronto in the early fifties, it was inevitable that I would hear the name Glenn Gould. I was born into a musical family: a piano family. My father, Jack, knew enough carpentry to help build a downstairs music studio where he taught piano lessons well into his late eighties. A certain amount of pioneering was involved in growing up in the suburbs those days. I remember picking through the bluish clay heaped up out of the house foundation to find the occasional arrowhead, which, of course, I threw away. Other houses were also rising up around us out of what once was Mississauga First Nation land. Our family became social. Over the months and years to follow, chatter about Gould intensified with week-end visits to our "place in the country" from other piano teachers or from friends with extensive record collections.

I was certainly not *au courant* on anything about Gould. Some of the adults had heard him play; their reports were confusing, to say the least.

I, on the other hand, had only heard *about* his playing. Having little access to the latest recordings was not that odd — these were still the days before classical music was played on FM radio (before there even was FM radio, in fact) and before hi-fi sets were a fixture in every modern rec room opposite a stack of LPs lining a lacquered maple cabinet.

Gould's name was often in the newspapers when I was a boy, yet, as I remember, the stories weren't always about his piano playing. He was

terrific at that, we all knew; but it seems he was also great at the art of becoming famous. Having such a celebrity in our midst in the early fifties was an exceptional thing. Canadians were uneasy about fame, particularly the homegrown type. Celebrity was something the Americans did better. The main exceptions were members of the royal family, hockey players, and the occasional politician or two (who were, of course, always compared to their American counterparts).

The Canadian rules didn't apply to Glenn Gould, we were learning. News of his rapid-fire conquest of the musical world was downright exciting. There was a Gould triumph here, a stunning breakthrough there. It

was like getting news of successful battles in a far-off war. Gould had Moscow at his feet; Leningrad, too. The Germans were overwhelmed. New York was blown away.

Later in the decade, when I'd begun to listen to him with more purpose and frequency, he already seemed a fixture in my life in much the way other things Canadian were, like Ted "Teeder" Kennedy, the stand-up captain of the hometown Toronto Maple Leafs, or the lovely hill on the golf course we tobogganed down in the dead dark after dinner.

Gould's still there, along with my memories of that hill. He refuses to budge from his place in my Canadian landscape. In my thinking Canada's

Canadian Centennial walk of fame, 1967 (left to right): Morley Callaghan, Sir Ernest MacMillan, Kate Reid, A.Y. Jackson, Glenn Gould, and Marshall McLuhan.

150th birthday in 2017 will be shared with what would have been Glenn Gould's eighty-fifth birthday.

Polls over the years regularly place Gould high on the list of the most famous Canadians. One can easily imagine him positioned for a group shot alongside any of the early prime ministers, everyone all bundled up — all good, overdressed, solid Canadian ancients. Gould would be a bit more rumpled than the rest, but every bit as steadfast.

(An aside: To me, *rumpled* is a loaded word because it has quite a history when it comes to Glenn Gould. In fact, the metamorphosis of Gould's "rumpled-ness" delineates his entire history. The accusation of being rumpled was from the start part of the accepted view of his eccentricities: Glenn Gould, the overconfident young guy from the sticks [Toronto], with his theatrically rumpled way of dressing: thick sweaters, gloves, scarves, hats, and, of course, a coat that looked less like something worn than something hovering around him like a thick fog. It was noted that "Gould arrived in coat, beret, muffler and gloves" at Columbia's 30th Street Studio in New York in June 1955 to record *The Goldberg Variations*, the hallmark of his amazingly uneven (read: rumpled) career. Gould's mid-career dishevelment — from the mid-sixties to the later seventies — could also be described as "multi-layered," and not just when it came to clothing.)

But back to my own piano playing for a moment. For the most part, I didn't think about it too deeply, sort of like a fish not having an opinion about water. When I did think about it years later, though, I realized that so much playing early in my life had made me monumentally inhospitable to the prospect of piano playing in the future. Sure, I owned albums — the early ones in the 78 rpm format — that focused on the lives of the great composers like Mozart and Schumann. But otherwise, piano music was as ubiquitous as the air in my teen years. My family's life when I was growing up was spent literally walking over the sounds of the piano, which floated up through the floorboards from the fingers of latest student pounding away at the old Heintzman in the basement.

By that time I'd heard Gould, but I hadn't really *listened*. Then one day the heavens opened — how else can I explain it? — and I saw the light. It wasn't about Gould, not at first. It was jazz that did it.

At least it started with jazz, when a high school friend about a year older loaned me a Benny Goodman LP that included the 1938 live recording of "Sing, Sing, Sing," which has always been known as the record with *the* Jess Stacy solo. That solo, about twelve or thirteen minutes long, comes partway through Goodman's now-famous 1938 Carnegie Hall concert. To begin, Stacy noodles around the keys for a moment, sampling the notes of the song's foundational A-minor chord before making the split-second decision to "come in real quiet," as he later described it. It is beautiful. The resulting solo's superb sense of proportion is evident when listening to the recording, with its sly references to Debussy and to Yiddish folk, yielding to Gospel and then … *to what?* Stacy turned a solo into an entire world.

Gould, though, was ambivalent toward jazz, although he respected its greatest technicians and tried playing some tunes over the years just to surprise his listeners. He also developed a friendship with the quietly cerebral jazz pianist Bill Evans later in his career, with whom he talked about the qualities of different pianos. But while Gould was never entirely comfortable with what jazz was about, some of his listeners, including me, knew he was not entirely separated from it or from any of the new non-classical kinds of piano playing that were out there. By the early sixties, when listening to Gould's *Goldberg* was a must-do, appreciating the piano also meant listening to Lennie Tristano and Oscar Peterson and Ray Charles. *Good Lord, Ray Charles!* Yes, looking back, I included Glenn Gould in that lineup. Jerry Lee Lewis, too.

Okay, I'm temporizing before digging deeper into the subject of Glenn Gould. Approaching the subject of Gould has never been easy and has probably scared some writers off. I feel I'm a bit of an outsider, at least when compared to the many people Gould worked with at the Canadian Broadcasting Corporation (CBC), the Stratford Festival, or wherever. (Gould got around, despite his reputation as the Prince of Privacy.) But I can't entirely let myself off the hook, because I followed his trail well before I was aware I was even on it, an accidental result of bad career planning on my part.

Growing up with music all around made me all the more determined to find a life that was somewhat distant from it. I was playing in rock and blues bands in my teens, but no matter: I'd had it with music, at least as a way of making a buck. I was determined to go in a different, non-musical direction. Oh, well. Things happen.

Thwarted in my determination — the different directions I mentioned weren't impressed at all by my marks in high school — I ended up back in music at the Royal Conservatory when Gould could still be found walking its halls. I eventually studied musicology at the University of Toronto under Harvey Olnick, the formidable lecturer who championed Gould to American music circles after the public debut of the *Goldbergs* in Toronto in 1954. Olnick rarely lacked certainty. Rocked by Gould's Toronto performance, he was absolutely sure of the great career that would follow (as he stated on more than one occasion). Olnick was spot-on when he compared Gould to Bohemian-American pianist Rudolf Serkin (as well as to Wanda Landowska) in an unsigned piece in *Musical Courier*, which would be Gould's debut in the American press. Serkin was the muscle-boy powerhouse of piano playing in these years, and this quality would have appealed to Olnick's bull-in-the-china-shop approach. To Olnick, Gould had a similar macho presence.

The first essay Harvey Olnick assigned to us asked us to consider the question "What is music?" After two years of wrestling with that question, I was led to a course in aesthetics taught by Geoffrey Payzant, an organist and University of Toronto philosophy professor. Payzant, who claimed to be able to identify any movement from any of Haydn's 106 symphonies, penned the book *Glenn Gould: Music and Mind*. The biography focused on Gould's way of thinking. Even Gould liked it, going so far as helping the author correct the proofs and select photographs. When asked to review the book for the *Globe and Mail*, Gould gave it a quiet rave.

Payzant and I talked on occasion as he was writing the book, although I was unaware of that fact at the time. Then he sent me a copy of the manuscript. "This book is not like the other books about pianists," it begins calmly. "How could it be? Gould is not like other pianists. He is a musical thinker who makes use of all available means to thought, including the piano." Few shorter or better summations of Gould had appeared before Payzant's book, or, perhaps, appeared after it.

By the early seventies I'd also crossed paths with Gould at the CBC, where I worked off and on in radio for some years. And as a music critic at the *Toronto Star* I interviewed him on a handful of occasions.

Approaching Glenn Gould in any guise is still intimidating. So much has been written already. So many experts. So many doctoral theses. So many opinions. So many books. So many books *about* other books. And so much of Gould's own writing about Glenn Gould. Tackling his recording legacy is another large-scale undertaking, which continues to grow increasingly monumental due to Sony Records' ongoing repackaging enterprises. (I've just come back from being given a peek at the latest iteration of *The Goldberg Variations,* which promises "The Complete Unreleased Recording Sessions, June 1955.")

Then there was the prerequisite visit to the Gould archives in Ottawa, Ontario. At Library and Archives Canada you're made aware of the vastness of the Gould holdings, which spread to yet another building (or two) in another part of town (who knows?). The unofficial king of the archives is Gould biographer Kevin Bazzana, who isn't on the library staff but seemingly knows more about the collection than some of the librarians. ("Well, Kevin says ..." was often the start of the answer to my questions.)

Bazzana, a music historian from British Columbia, authored *Wondrous Strange: The Life and Art of Glenn Gould,* the research-rich 2004 biography. He told me there was a lot more to find in the archives; I think he meant this as encouragement. Gould's Canadian intimates like *Wondrous Strange* because they feel it brings the appropriate Canadian spin to what they felt was the "Americanization" of their man in the more mainstream Gould biography, *Glenn Gould: A Life in Variations,* published in 1990 by Otto Friedrich, formerly of the *Saturday Evening Post* and *Time.*

This Canadian-American divide on Gould is not to be dismissed, although the Canadian concern about Friedrich's take is overstated, in my opinion. Gould's Canadian-ness is impossible for anyone to ignore or dilute. If Gould were a fictional figure — as he did emerge in his own writing and broadcasting — he might in my mind be compared to F. Scott Fitzgerald's Jay Gatsby, whose longing for the American dream went nowhere because the dream had come and gone before he had the goods to make it his own. "I was reminded of something," Gatsby says when thinking out loud of his passion for Daisy, the love of his early life, "an elusive rhythm, a fragment of lost words, that I heard somewhere a long time ago." Gould is Gatsby's opposite; he realized his dream at all costs. Gould found there was a boundless future for him.

Reckoning with Gould's mystical side can also be intimidating. So, too, the bedrock of Ontario Christianity that marked his upbringing. He was never far from a Bible, we're told; but rarely did he quote from it.

Gould dealt with his ongoing physical misery, real or imagined (the difference seemed to mean little to him), much the way a man might have to deal with a demanding, petulant mistress who could nag him to distraction (or to a hotel during a 1958 European tour).

"My hysteria about eating," he said in 1955, "it's getting worse all the time."

In 1956 he's taking anti-psychotic medications like Thorazine, as well as reserpine, another anti-psychotic, though it is also taken to lower blood pressure.

In 1959 people are spying on him, he reports. He says he hears voices.

Most interpretive disagreements regarding Gould begin with what's found, or not found, in a diary he maintained throughout 1977 into early 1978, which is thick with his notations about things going wrong. With regard to pain, he wrote on June 23: "For the last several days right wrist had been unbearably sore after any 10–15-minute practice session."

A reading of these entries led Frank R. Wilson, an American neurologist, to write a 2000 article suggesting that things were wrong with Gould from the very start; that "for virtually his entire career, Gould struggled against and adroitly finessed critical limitation in upper body, forearm, and hand movement." Focal dystopia, the term for this condition, indicates abnormal hand and finger functioning. In Gould's case, it suggested certain fingers tended to bunch in certain ways, minimizing how broadly he might be able to stretch out his thumb and fifth finger. When I went through some of his annotated scores, with correct fingers listed below each note, I noticed a lot of middle fingers were used. A professional-grade pianist I asked to look over it said his fingering was very odd indeed.

Gould-inspired work created since the pianist's death in 1982 has taken on a life and dimension of its own. The Gould effect and legacy now occupy our minds as much as his immediate history. I would cite David Young's play *Glenn* and François Girard's *Thirty Two Short Films About Glenn Gould* as excellent examples. His *Goldberg Variations* alone have had a significant afterlife — witness Canadian composer Christos Hatzis's *Gouldberg Variations* or Richard Powers's short story *The Gold Bug Variations*. Canadian-born French author Nancy Huston's *Les Variations Goldberg*

His score, his scribbles.

offers what is perhaps the most transgressive take on the Bach, when in one early scene of her Paris-based novel the variation in question is sexual.

Arguably the most audacious Gould *Goldberg* riff is *The Goldberg Variations: Aria, BMV 988, Johann Sebastian Bach, 1741,* Canadian artist Tim Lee's deconstruction of a film of Gould's *Goldberg* performance where Gould's hands are shown on monitors positioned near enough to each other to give the impression the hands belong to the viewer. Karaoke Glenn Gould.

Gould's speech to the Royal Conservatory of Music's 1964 graduation class, where he speaks of "the inner ear," led to *The Inner Eye,* a series of quasi-surreal, magic-realist collages by Vancouver artist Joan McCrimmon.

Gould's *Goldbergs* have become the fault-line of his legacy with following generations of piano players. Acclaimed Austrian pianist, poet, and author Alfred Brendel famously hated it. Another Austrian, Jörg Demus, who recorded his own *Goldberg Variations,* used the word *detest* when I mentioned Gould's version to him. Angela Hewitt, a Canadian Bach specialist, questioned Gould's Bach — "it's more about him than Bach" — but recognized how his playing as a young man "was totally fearless, there's a ferocity, a youthful exuberance." Other pianists suggest Gould's greatest legacy might go beyond his performances. Jon Kimura Parker, the Canadian pianist and professor of piano performance, told me he urges his students to follow Gould's beyond-the-piano thinking. Still others — the fine Italian pianist Francesco Piemontesi, mentored by Brendel, for example — thinks Gould's embrace of technology opened the eyes of other pianists.

The fact that a Bach prelude and fugue played by Gould is hurtling into infinity on the 1977 *Voyager* spaceship amazed earlier biographers. These days many would be surprised if it was proven that Gould *wasn't* being heard somewhere in space.

And so it's gone. Hollywood tapped Gould most notably when Hannibal Lecter in *Silence of the Lambs* wanted Gould's *Goldbergs* but was served the same piece in the film score by pianist Jerry Zimmerman. Years ago, during my day as a film critic, I heard of plans for Gould to be the soundtrack for a Sly Stallone movie, a decision abandoned along the way.

And writers? There are books channelling Gould for kids, for young adults, and for fellow obsessives — any of Austrian author Thomas Bernhard's novels *Der Untergeher* (translated as *The Loser* in English) or *Alte Meister*, or his play *Heldenplatz*, for example. French comic book artist Sandrine Revel's 2015 illustrated biography, *Glenn Gould: une vie à contretemps*, resolves many of Gould's apparent contradictions into a very human story.

But something deeper is going on. There's a sea change in the nature of Gould's afterlife that can't be ignored. He has new listeners, ones lacking any standard order classical music training or any shared history with Gould. They hear his playing differently, understand his history differently, and respond differently to him and his music.

Early Gould commentary, arriving during his life or soon after his death, had, like Gould's own thinking, its basis solidly in the Protestant/ European traditions and cultural practices extending to musicology and musical practice. Commentary from and about alternative traditions, non-male, non-white, and non-European, for starters, didn't figure much early on in the Gould legacy.

Even the very idea of musical progress — such atonality — took place within Eurocentric terms in Gould's mind. His fascination with technology, which might have been his exit from the traditional, only tightened his embrace on tradition. Technology allowed Gould to stay Gould; to stay distant, in control, ordered. Order was being challenged in the world well beyond his St. Clair Avenue apartment, roiling with unprecedented, society-changing manifestations: Black/Gay/Feminist/Bi/Transgendered power, plugging and tuning in and turning on. No matter. All the while Gould was excitedly imagining how to reach "the enormous audience" that might result from technology's "creation of a new and paradoxical condition of privacy."

Yet this new thinking about Gould comes, in its way, from some constraints of his own past. Emerging artists are messing with Gould's sombre mythology. Some are even parodying his piano playing: Catch *Glenn Gould Plays "Invaria" by John Oswald* on YouTube. Oswald, a Toronto-based composer-artist, reconfigures a previously filmed sequence of Gould playing, so that the notes of Oswald's own piece,

Invaria, appear to be played by Gould. On YouTube he gets hits like a rock star.

Gould's two *Goldbergs* feel like background music throughout Madeleine Thien's 2016 novel *Do Not Say We Have Nothing.* Various Gould attributes crop up here and there in the story, such as when the narrator's father, Kai-Jiang, drifts back to memories of himself as a famous concert pianist in China: he would hum along with a Glenn Gould recording, all the while pretending to conduct. I came to realize that Thien, who played the 1955 *Goldbergs* daily while she was writing the book in Berlin, was measuring her story to create an overarching continuity down to its very paragraphs, the same way that Gould himself uncovered Bach's hidden continuity in his second *Goldberg* recording (1981).

I came to write about this new sense of Gould by catching his refraction in what's called popular culture and in the continuation of so-called classical culture. This book came to life with its feet in both camps. This had a lot to do with Leonard Cohen, the ninth laureate of the Glenn Gould Prize in 2012, and the piece I was asked to contribute to that evening's gala. It started — the piece, I mean, not the gala — with my suggesting how much poet and pianist had in common beyond their unique singing. Aloneness was an obvious trait, of course: a sun-drenched Cohen writing alone in Hydra "on a table set among the rocks"; a meditative Gould going unnoticed sitting in a Toronto park.

I had met Cohen over the years in my role as a rock critic/journalist and could not help but be reminded how much like Gould he was in certain ways. Gould and Cohen themselves had met only once, and that was in 1963 when Cohen, cash-strapped as only a poet can be, took an assignment from *Holiday* magazine to interview Gould about the world's cities. The meeting took place in Ottawa, where Cohen remembers being so transfixed by what Gould was saying that he forgot to take notes, thus leaving the piece unwritten along with his reactions to meeting the famous pianist.

Understand one and you understand the other: that was my thinking as I wrote. I noted how alike they were in their ability to go famously unnoticed. Both had a thing about overcoats. Both cultivated the role of Mysteriously Bundled Figure Silhouetted Against Bleak Canadian

Landscape, their mutual riffing on Northrop Frye's observation about Canada being a "cool climate for heroes." Both questioned their faith.

"I believe in God," Gould once said, "Bach's God."

"When it comes to lamentations," Cohen once wrote, "I prefer Aretha Franklin to, let's say, Leonard Cohen."

Both men grew enormously famous by claiming to avoid fame. And I knew from experience both could be funny, right?

Right, said Gould's people.

Cohen's protectors weren't so sure. They weren't sure being funny was right for the occasion. They didn't want to "upset" him.

So the piece was a no go. That meant stop.

This book is a new start.

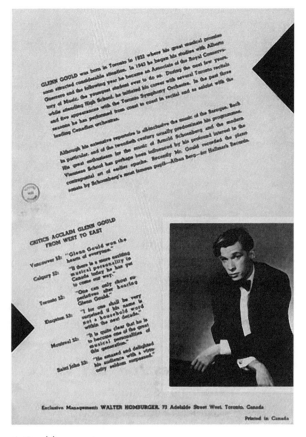

A Gould concert program.

CHAPTER ONE

The Enigma's Variations

A little more practice is in order.

> — Glenn Gould, New York, June 1955,
> while recording *The Goldberg Variations*

I often wonder about what people new to Glenn Gould, or those who only know his name, think when they come upon the life-size sculpture of the pianist outside the Canadian Broadcasting Centre in Toronto for the first time. Perhaps they wonder what exactly the artist is saying about him as they observe how the afternoon light on the folds of the surface make Gould's clothing look as sleek as silk. This part of the city is about crowds and conventions and baseball fans and fun and chain restaurants. It's not designed for thoughtfulness. Still, it's possible. Me, I can imagine the unthinkable stretches of empty space beyond this point as I hear the trains heading east and west; once that was about all that brought anyone down to this part of town — the Canadian National and Canadian Pacific Railways. Those who know about such things know that the CN and CP were Canada's first radio broadcasters and aired the first music show back in the days when the CBC was still on a drawing board.

I also think about the father of the jazz great Oscar Peterson, who was once a porter on one of those trains running out of Montreal. I

Equipped.

Timeless.

remember also the Festival Express, the mobile Canadian Woodstock with car after car jammed with rock stars and wannabes heading out of town, one great collective raggedy-ass party, going west and even deeper into sixties mythology.

Gould and Peterson never played together, although both said they thought about it. But Gould knew about Janis Joplin, who was on the Festival Express. He included her song "Mercedes-Benz" alongside Bach and simple hymns in *The Quiet in the Land*, his 1977 radio documentary about Mennonite life.

I think of my father, stopping a bit west of here with me, so that I could get out of the car to see a bit of the city before I went on to my piano lesson at the Royal Conservatory of Music, then at the corner of College Street and University Avenue, since moved to Bloor Street.

Canadian sculptor Ruth Abernethy's *Glenn* offers up a solid, handsome icon that reminds us that the slumped figure was taller in life than is often remembered. The work catches many signature Gould tics: he seems bent into the bench itself just as he melded with his piano stool; his right hand on his cap gives the impression it might fly off at any moment in a gust of Front Street wind; and his expression proclaims a stagey seriousness that might be, maybe, just a little over the top. "Hmm, yes, but, ah, speaking, as well one might, in Schoenbergian terms …"

You can practically hear a professorial Gould muttering on and on pedantically like this as visitor after visitor sits next to the master, deliciously aware that their rendezvous is a camera-ready setup.

Theatre is the key. It's my theme, in a way. It was Gould's theme, too. Media awareness: the star knowing where the camera was, where the microphone was. A familiar enough figure on Toronto streets back in the day, Gould could be found performing his own hobo lumpy young/old guy act, padded against the wind as if in a wintry battle scene in a vintage Soviet movie. Walking can be a subversive act, particularly if done with intent. And it certainly was for Gould, private and purposeful all at once. *Where's he going? What's he thinking?* might be questions people asked as he passed. *What's that he's humming?* This memory is now only the property of old-timers, and they're unlikely to be walking those same streets as often — if they still exist at all, those streets.

Glenn Gould is always in motion in my lasting memories of him, although these images are always in black and white, like the National Film Board newsreels we were shown at school before any of our parents had a TV. Film rolling from the early fifties, when I might see him charging through the halls of the old Royal Conservatory of Music — "the Con," as my father, a teacher there, called it. He was hugely famous just about everywhere in the world already, but not here, not really, as the rest of us struggled away with our iffy talents in cold practice rooms. I remember seeing him in the Con's tiny cafeteria arguing away with someone, people coming up and talking to him. It's still black and white in my memory from almost twenty years later, in the early 1970s, when I'd find myself crossing Glenn Gould's path late in the afternoon around the old CBC building on Jarvis Street, where I worked for some years. In these memories, and in retelling them, I can't simply say "Gould" — it's too detached from the way one felt about him — but certainly not "Glenn" as in "Hey, Glenn." It had to be Glenn Gould.

We met a few times — he remembered I'd interviewed him on more than one occasion — and we'd stop on the street or in a hall and talk

*N*OT LONG AFTER *Glenn Gould's death, Toronto artist Joanne Tod began a series of paintings dedicated to Gould, one showing the pianist looking grim-faced and hunched over the keyboard of a black grand piano — looking as long and menacing as a mob boss's limousine (see dust jacket).*

"I called my painting Idiot Savant,*" says Tod. "It's fixed within the context of the work I was doing at the time, which was to have ironic, double-meaning titles. His* Goldberg Variations *had been my introduction to the classical music genre — a classicism that sort of dove-tailed with my interest at the time in Manet — so there was some resonance there with him that I wanted to portray. But there were his eccentricities to account for, his 'idiot-savantry,' if you wish. I think he's kind of hip, too. He's wearing those long, pointed shoes. He has longish hair. If I'd known all about his bad habits I would have made him hot meals."*

for a bit about what he was doing. One really late night at the CBC he appeared at the door of the second- or third-floor editing room I was using, startling me — "Like a ghost," I told him.

I bet he liked that. The setting was right. The top-floor rooms in the old CBC building — offices, edit suites, storage, whatever else was there — had the murk and crannies found in attics in horror flicks. This added a little extra *frisson* for those lovers creeping upstairs for a late-night boff.

"And what are you working on?" he asked, moving close enough to peer over my shoulder. I don't remember now — probably a segment of a breezy morning show, *The Scene*, he himself would contribute to.

I flattened a length of tape against the tiny metal block, cutting it at an angle with my razor blade, in the narrow slot provided. After another cut in different place on the tape, I brought the two pieces together.

"You realize, of course, that process will be taken over by a machine," Gould said, straightening up.

"Probably," I said. "But it won't be as much fun."

Tape splicing — replaced now by the digital edit suite, the MIDI (Musical Instrument Digital Interface) and other goodies — had its own set of quirky tools, including a marker of some sort to indicate where to splice a tape as well as a razor blade held in a special metal clamp to do the splicing, plus tape to piece the parts together. Veteran editors with eyes as sharp as diamond cleavers could fuse together two halves of the identical note recorded at different times with one of their fine tape splices. Gould's editing prowess was a legend around the CBC. Indeed, as the years went on he seemed far more interested in extolling some frightfully complex bit of tape splicing he'd finished than his latest recording. A listener asked by Gould to guess the number of edits or splices in a finished documentary would inevitably guess far fewer splices than were there.

I now realize that Gould probably did little actual cutting on his own, especially after Columbia producer Andrew Kazdin's revelations years later that he did the actual editing when recording with Gould, with Gould hovering around in an advisory capacity.

With me, though, Gould seemed stalled on the word *fun*.

"Less fun maybe," he said, "but a logical step, a very human step, too — the step toward perfection — if you think of it."

We talked a bit more and then he drifted away, leaving me to whiz strips of magnetic tape backward and forward, searching for the right spot to splice.

REVIVING THE CORPS

The CBC's English-language headquarters on Front Street is now home to the Glenn Gould Studio. The 340-seat theatre opened in 1993, eleven years after Gould's death. It's only one of several places around town with his name attached, most notably the Glenn Gould Professional School at the glassy new Royal Conservatory of Music. There's also a Glenn Gould Park at the northwest corner of St. Clair Avenue and Avenue Road, with its statue of Peter Pan — entirely fitting for the boy-man Gould kept alive long after he was no longer a child. And I imagine the number of plaques bearing his name will increase with every new Gould connection that's discovered by cities and towns he passed through for some project or another: Orillia, Wawa, North York …

All things associated with Gould have taken on a life of their own over the years, becoming almost totemic, fetish objects. Stories about his beloved Steinway CD 318 fill one book. How long before there's a monograph on his familiar chair, bent like a Picasso sculpture? Somewhere stored away in one basement or another are the Gould family cottage shutters, much desired by Gould fans still looking for mementos.

The CBC statue, owned by the Glenn Gould Foundation, is different. It fixes this intensely private person forever in public. It places Gould in a different sort of space, a more public space where Gould is lesser known, if known at all — a place he himself would not have been ready for. Sculptor Abernethy's roots in the theatre working with props and the like are apparent in Gould's caught-in-motion pose. It's almost as if he is impatiently waiting for a stranger to sit opposite him and talk. Ironically (the word *irony* hovers over everything Gould), his companions might be Toronto Blue Jays fans on their way to the nearby Rogers Centre, unaware of Gould's dislike of competition. One can imagine the day when the majority of those strangers will be as much in the dark about Gould or what he did as are most tourists in Paris walking along Avenue du Général Leclerc unaware that its namesake was revered by generations of French as the liberator of Paris.

As with Abernethy's sculpture, Gould, the idea, the subject, is always in motion, too. The Gould canon, a sizable enough collection while he was alive, has grown impressively in the years since his death in 1982. I've never heard anyone say, "Why, yes, I have a book on Glenn Gould." It's always, "I have several — well, quite a few actually." But as Gould is discovered by a new generation of academics — the majority not around when he rocketed to world fame in the mid-1950s, and unencumbered by any personal contact with him — many are apt to see him in the broader context of popular culture. I've seen his name associated with the word *hipster* on occasion, and I get why, although I'm certain Gould himself would not. How else do you describe a brilliant recluse with shaggy hair who loved to drive big, shiny American cars out in the restless night, his pockets stuffed with uppers and downers, the radio picking up sad songs?

Those who are curious about Glenn Gould and dig deeper might be taken aback by just how many Gould narratives there are. The reason for this, of course, is his protean productivity on so many fronts: his recordings, wide-ranging in content and almost unrivalled in number; his intelligence and restless inquisitiveness, made public via his radio and TV appearances; his written essays and their rococo convolutions; and the logic-defying contradictions of his life. All of these aspects of Gould's life have given rise to any number of narrative approaches. Hence, the themes-and-variations method for organizing any account of Gould, such as Otto Friedrich's early biography, *Glenn Gould: A Life and Variations*, or *Thirty Two Short Films About Glenn Gould*, François Girard's episodic film biography, or Georges Leroux's *Partita for Glenn Gould*, whose introductory section, "Praeludium," is followed by a "Toccata" then an "Allemande" and so on in musical fashion.

Ever the control freak, throughout his life Gould allowed the public, friends, and even lovers only glimpses of the private Gould. Over the years he left rooms full of scribbled sheets behind — notes, lists, one revision after another revision, the good revealed here, the bad there, but almost never anything one could consider reflective, overall. On July 30, 1952, when Gould was filling out his biographical data sheet at the CBC, he left answers to many of the questions blank. After *What is your favourite amusement?* Blank. After *What was the most dramatic moment of your career?* Blank. *Under what circumstances do you like to prepare your program?* Blank. *What attracted you to radio?* Blank. Blank for first audition. Blank for current programs. Blank for current sport. Blank. Blank. Blank.

GOULDS GALORE

Many believe the Gould enigma is one code that is not likely to be cracked — a view encouraged by Gould himself. It accounts for the paucity of intimate personal detail in his voluminous notes about, say, his love life, for just one instance. Peter F. Ostwald, the German-born American violinist/psychiatrist who counselled Gould as a friend over the years, called this the "diffusion of Gould's identity" in *Glenn Gould: The Ecstasy and Tragedy of Genius*, a startling portrait of the artist in rapid decline. In the womb-like atmosphere of the radio studio, Ostwald says, Gould went through "a certain loss of the primary image of himself as a pianist, an image that had been built up in childhood under his mother's guidance."

The narrative of Gould that's best known focuses on his career highs and lows: the discovery of a brilliant pianist whose 1955 recording of Bach's *The Goldberg Variations* may well be the greatest classical recording of all time; then, watching as the freaky artist walks away from a multi-million-dollar career. And, well … that's it. Well, not entirely. This particular narrative is enriched by circumstances surrounding his 1981 *Goldberg* recording, its autumnal atmosphere seemingly foreshadowing his death a year later.

The second narrative, Glenn Gould as one of the twentieth century's great pianists, is of concern to a distressingly diminishing number of classical music cognoscenti. While generally impressed by the volume and scope of Gould's recording activities, they remain unimpressed by what they feel is the inconsistency of its quality. They will point to senior elite pianists, from Vladimir Ashkenazy to Anton Kuerti, who insist that many of Gould's performances are flat out wrongheaded. Several composers of works performed by Gould — the Czech-Canadian Oskar Morawetz, for example — have asserted the same thing: that Gould ignored basic musical signage to swerve off-road and do his own thing. Then there are the bootlegs of live concerts, and rumours about tapes of private recordings.

Story three: call it "Glenn Gould: YouTube Star." Watching Gould live, still exhilarating, leaves still more unanswered questions. The narrative of Gould's brief, incendiary, fretful, problematic, erratic, and eventually discontinued concert career — I mean the story of the concerts themselves before and after his dramatic early visit to the Soviet Union — may well constitute the greatest Glenn Gould unknown of them all, one that transcended his growing awareness of discomfort — psychological, physical, and aesthetic — with the process.

The fourth story (major film potential here) concerns the private, sexual Glenn Gould. This topic has seemingly lost its intrigue, having been exposed to some degree by Michael Clarkson, a journalist (and one-time *Toronto Star* colleague of mine) who established that Cornelia Foss, even while married to composer Lukas Foss, remained Gould's mistress until his idiosyncrasies drove her back to her composer husband. Gould's earlier historians tended to turn a blind eye to Gould's sex

Moody blue.

life — well, some of them peeped, but only a little — even though Gould didn't avoid discussing sex in his writing and thinking and yearning for Petula Clark and Barbra Streisand. That Gould might be gay has gained even less traction, although throughout his life he liked to have a guy pal, a buddy, close at his side, whether it was Ray Roberts, his hired factotum or Lorne Tulk, whom Gould considered a brother. As with some other artists — Goya, Mozart, Miles Davis, Dylan — turbulence in Gould's private life seems to have energized his imagination. It was against the background of the disintegration of his life with Cornelia and her two children that Gould was at his most productive and, in public, his most upbeat.

Story five explores Gould and Peter Pan, or more so Gould *as* Peter Pan. Gould didn't cling to his childhood as much as it clung to him. He lived with his parents in their city home into his thirties, and he would repeatedly over the years retreat to the family cottage and memories from his childhood. He was close with his cousin, Jessie Greig, seven years older, who lived with the Goulds in Toronto while she went to teacher's college. But the chilling of his friendship with Robert Fulford, his next door neighbour as a kid, left something missing in his later life, although that happened when they were both older, as Fulford points out, and were living radically different lives: Fulford by then was married with children, Gould an international music superstar.

Then there are the animals in his life. The first major news stories about him show him surrounded by his menagerie of pets. His last letter is about his abiding love of animals. One of his legacies is his gift to the Humane Society in Toronto. And the most beautifully lunatic moment — one I love him for more than any other — is when he tried to get a pack of watchful pachyderms to sing in German at the Toronto Zoo in 1978, in a scene appearing in the documentary film *Glenn Gould's Toronto*.

Anyone writing about Gould needs to understand that whatever direction he or she takes, it is likely to lead to Gould having been there first. Once you've rounded this or that corner in some narrative, have solved this or that puzzle — or not — you'll likely find he's been there to elucidate in his words what you have just discovered. But not always. Because sometimes Gould buried the truth, unconsciously or deliberately, or somewhere in between; Gould's archived scribbles and notes fill entire rooms in Ottawa, but the majority of their contents are clues, not revelations.

This particular Gould, the unfathomable artist, has a particular following. "He is our ideal of the disembodied artist, the pure intellect," writes Kevin Wood in the liner notes of an early 1990s compilation recording called *Glenn Gould's Greatest Hits: Highlights from the Glenn Gould Collection*, produced and marketed by one Kevin Wood. And yes, it's true: elusiveness is a distinguishing characteristic of many historical classical geniuses. Wood points to Franz Liszt as an earlier example (although I'd hardly describe anyone selling his fans vials of his bath water for them to sip at rapturously, as Liszt did, as "elusive"): "The enigma of Gould is different; for him, there is no historical memory, no mystical tradition."

Gould knew early on there was something very, very specific about him, something he'd later understand had historical antecedents. Glenn Gould's many epiphanies — the music of Fartein Valen, the Norwegian Christian mystic, for example — started early on with understanding his own genius. The word *genius* seems inopportune now, best worked around or avoided because of its overuse in describing middling talents. Gould himself used the word, but almost exclusively to describe others. Yet there it was, this unfathomable talent. And he knew it.

He hated to be described as a *prodigy*. Gould rejected that designation his entire life. He knew about prodigies, of course. He grew up hearing about and performing Mozart as musical wunderkind. The first concert he was taken to by his parents — he was just six years old — was by Polish-born pianist Josef Hofmann. Hofmann had been acclaimed as a child prodigy, having given his first concert when he was only five.

There was something slick and superficial in the very idea of the prodigy. In an era of kid wonders, perky little simpletons showing off on amateur-hour shows on radio, Glenn was winning kudos playing serious music at serious music festivals. He had raw potential — at least he'd heard his mother brag about this raw potential. She also spoke of his unbelievably retentive memory, about his sense of perfect pitch that allowed him to sing a precise note without hearing it first. So, early on he knew he was part of a serious undertaking. He believed and trusted in his mother when she said he was on his way to something big, but all in due time. But due time was rapid-paced for both of them. The pages in the beginner music books young Glenn Gould was

With Mozart — the budgie.

given, typical of the sort all children are given when they're starting out, are remarkably pristine, as if each page needed to be open for just the shortest time.

Soon enough, Glenn Gould came across the craziest understanding about himself — or rather, about his abilities. Every school everywhere felt it had its own musical genius in its midst. It was the same with every community, every small rural town. And in each and every instance, the belief was that their kid genius was the one and only.

But Glenn Gould knew it was true only of him. He was that kid.

But I am also interested in another sort of epiphany and in a different narrative of Glenn Gould, which, in my estimation, embraces all others: his role in the creation of Glenn Gould, media star, media manipulator, and Canadian intellectual icon.

Not entirely unnoticed by earlier biographers, this instinct of Gould's has been downplayed for reasons I understand. The motivation for Gould's media reinvention of himself had been in place since childhood — he had dreams of being a broadcaster well before he achieved international acclaim as a quirky concert star — and this dream shaped many of his crucial decisions. The attention he attracted — and he both wanted and needed it — by way of his piano playing connected him directly to the burgeoning new world of innovative technologies, bringing the wired city together far more so than roads ever did. Gould became the singular source of a singular signal to be found on LPs, or FM radio, or hi-fi.

The piano, for all its polyphonic potential, in his thinking, was nevertheless designed for acoustic spaces, spaces increasingly unused or unwanted — front parlours once meant for entertaining, saloons, silent movie houses, and, yes, concert halls. In these orphaned spaces, he saw that pianos were becoming another form of furniture, needing polishing as much as tuning. But not yet for Glenn Gould. Not quite yet. For him, the piano was an extension of himself, like an artificial organ connecting past practices with the new. He played the piano and played *through* the piano to reach his true objective — the transference of sound into impulse and back into sound again.

> All this complication of oxygen tubes, heating equip-
> ment; these speaking tubes that form this "intercom"
> running between the members of the crew. This mask
> through which I breathe. I am attached to the plane by
> a rubber tube as indispensable as an umbilical cord.
> Organs have been added to my being, and they seem to
> intervene between me and my heart.
> — *Flight to Arras*, Antoine de Saint-Exupéry

MEDIA IS THE MESSAGE

Gould as the consummate media performer/subject/manipulator has not gone unrecognized, but has been downplayed. Gould "The TV Star" is a chapter heading in one book; "Vaudevillian" is the title in another. Lorne Tulk, one of Gould's friends and technicians over the years, thinks Gould was fascinated by singer Petula Clark due to her ability to market herself. A number of Gould critics, and not a few admirers, have remarked on how adeptly he handled stardom.

"Can you think of another pianist who had such strong contact with contemporary media, who was so able to use them, to control them, and to make them serve his own ends?" asked French journalist and music-ologist Jacques Drillon. "In the twentieth century, the artist without media is nothing." Drillon was depressed at the thought. He might well have been encouraged.

Van Cliburn, Sviatoslav Richter, and Arturo Benedetti Michelangeli were Gould's pianist rivals for a time, a type of rivalry that he disparaged in public and but never lost sight of. Before last-minute replacement of the suddenly vexatious Michelangeli for a CBC recording session of Beethoven's *Emperor Concerto*, Gould reportedly said, "Just think that the Number One pianist is substituting for the Number Two."

Seen from outside the somewhat conservative world of classical music, Gould might be said to have more in common with postmodernist writers or visual artists, where art's production had yielded to interest in art's reproduction (Robert Rauschenberg's migration from assemblages to silk screens; Gould's from live performance to entire reconstructions via editing). John Rea, a leading Montreal composer and teacher of com-position at McGill University, points out that less than a decade after the 1955 release of *The Goldberg Variations*, there appeared an early Warhol silkscreen, *Thirty Are Better Than One*, consisting of a grid of multiple images of the *Mona Lisa*, most likely a comment on the grid of multiple Gould images on the famous *Goldberg* album cover, with Gould talking about the music but not shown performing.

Gould fashioned a beloved media figure out of his manufactured multiple personas. In this regard he rivalled Marshall McLuhan's love of performing and media-readiness. For many artists the media was the new performance space.

John Cage, who once appeared on prime time American TV as a benevolent Zen dreamer, had funny ideas about what music was. Cage's and Gould's paths crossed on occasion, and Cage's ideas were never entirely off Gould's radar. For Cage, an *idea* could be performed, not only notes or sound. His forty-minute *Lecture on Nothing* contains the famous line: "I have nothing to say and I am saying it and that is poetry as I need it." Based on the notion that art can never be possessed, it would have rattled the possessive Gould. (Elsewhere, Cage says: "Slowly, as the talk goes on, we are getting nowhere and that is a pleasure.") Gould didn't always get Cage, but nevertheless he wanted the American composer as part of the lineup for his Arnold Schoenberg documentary. In a letter he wrote to Cage to ask him to contribute to the project, Gould acknowledged that he knew Cage's feelings about Schoenberg were "perhaps rather ambivalent." In fact, Schoenberg and Cage operated on different musical planets, which Gould well knew.

However, Gould and Cage held in common a deep-rooted understanding of music's potential to be the soundtrack for political upheaval and radical change. Cage's *4'33"* is three movements of silence — or rather, four minutes and thirty-three seconds during which a pianist doesn't play a single note, leaving the audience to listen to its own sound: its own music, as it were. Cage's "dismantling of the hierarchy between musical sound in particular and sound in general" was "arguably the single most decisive influence on our current preoccupation with the sonic environment as a suppressed but vital aspect of the social world," observed American art critic Ina Blom in her 2010 *ArtForum* review of *The Anarchy of Silence: John Cage and Experimental Art* at the Museu d'Art Contemporani de Barcelona in 2009. Gould, by turning his back on what he called the "penitentiary sentence" of being a touring concert artist, offered a radical alternative to the entire classical music apparatus and its insistence on the hierarchical superiority of the live concert. Gould, like Cage, understood the enormous power in silence; Gould just meant his own. (One is also reminded that musical "revolutions" have an extra-musical framework. Beethoven, arguably the first indie classical artist, understood that musical independence meant following the money, more easily found with the burgeoning mobile middle classes than with the politically vulnerable aristocracy.)

Back to the statue for a minute. Each Gould narrative is located where it should be. Abernethy's statue places Gould's media being at the CBC, which was home to him — another home. He had a desk at the CBC Radio offices. He sent letters on CBC letterhead, correspondence to fans from Bloomington to Auckland or to Madame Pablo Casals. As a return address he gave CBC Radio's, 354 Jarvis Street. He kidded with the chatty ladies in the basement cafeteria: they were more likely the reason he was there than the food itself. Some nights when he was working on something, he could be found pacing up and down the CBC corridors, his very own version of Batman, coat flapping. A story I heard during my days there was how Gould, on a whim, intended to fill in for a newsreader when the one on the schedule was late turning up. He understood — he *felt* — his CBC audience, a crowd already familiar with his lightly mocking tone, his role-playing, his quirks and prejudices and love of words. There's an intimacy there.

As well, the statue remains resolutely in the present tense through the varied, unpredictable, yet inevitably joyful interactions people have with it, a contrast with the image of him in his final years, with everyone hearing more and more reports of his poor health, torn soul, wrecked body, nighthawk hours, unfulfilled loves, and sunken dreams.

The last time I was passing by the CBC — when music was on my mind and not the Jays' relief pitching (the building's nearness to Toronto's baseball stadium notwithstanding) — what I found myself thinking about wasn't any of Gould's iconic recordings — the Brahms Intermezzi, say — but his late-sixties recording of Liszt's transcription of Beethoven's Fifth Symphony. This playing could've made the rock 'n' roll charts because it's soaked in show business swagger and sweat, starting with the motor-rhythmic drive worthy of Oscar Peterson riffing at full throttle right from the signature *Da da da — DUM* opening. ("You are too dumb," Beethoven is supposed to have said when asked about the meaning of the opening.) And something more: the Beethoven is another crazily brilliant choice on Gould's part, a retro choice given that playing transcriptions died out when the arrival of recording gave everyone the chance to hear the real thing. Cheeky, this.

Chilly Gonzales sure understands. The energetic jazz pianist shows his love for Gould in a YouTube tribute for Gould's birthday. This passion, as Gonzales points out, is a love of caricature and parody, "the superficial aspect" of Gould, who "paved the way" for other generations of eccentric piano geniuses. Gonzales is talking about Gonzales, of course, he of the Gould-like emerging paunch and receding hairline. But he's also channelling Gould's own practice of self-parody. In Gould's liner notes for his recording of the Fifth — written by a Gould seemingly connecting with his inner tweedy Brit music critic — he writes: "Mr. Gould has been absent from British platforms these past few years and if this new CBS release is indicative of his current musical predilections perhaps it is just as well."

Gonzales's Gould riff is not isolated either. Young deejays are remixing Gould tracks. YouTube surfers are blown away listening to the relentless, heartbreaking attack of Gould's strafing technique. Gould's name pops up in rock star interviews from the likes of Neil Young and producer Bob Ezrin and Patti Smith. The latter claims "a deep, abstract relationship with him. You can feel his mind."

Discovering Gould is an ongoing adventure on the internet. I came across a posted vignette that sounds so much like Gould. The story came from a piece that appeared originally in the September 1998 issue of *Hemispheres*, United Airlines' in-flight magazine. It's by an American writer, Barbara Abercrombie, and she describes the last months of her mother's life. When she went into the hospital, Abercrombie says, "I bought her a CD player and she listened to Glenn Gould's Beethoven piano sonatas over and over. But she wasn't just listening; she was working — figuring out how to improve her own playing. 'I play this part too fast,' she said. 'Oh, listen to how he does it.'"

CHAPTER TWO

Altered Egos

April 1, 1951, 8:00 p.m. EST

MAX FERGUSON (THE ANNOUNCER): We hope you enjoy *Startime*!

ORCHESTRA: THEME UP FULL … FADE … HOLD

FERGUSON: Every Sunday evening, the trans-Canada network of the CBC brings you *Startime* … an hour of entertainment especially designed to please the families of Canada …

ORCHESTRA: THEME UP FULL AND OUT

FERGUSON: Tonight Paul Scherman conducts the *Startime* orchestra and chorus … and our guests are the brilliant young soprano Lois Marshall … the European tenor Joseph Reiner … popular singer Norma Locke … and pianist Glenn Gould. And, as usual, the man who tells you all about the stars and the music is your *Startime* host, Frank Willis.

WILLIS: Although Glenn Gould is only eighteen — a fifth-form student at high school — he's considered one of Canada's most accomplished concert pianists....

Now, with the *Startime* orchestra, Glenn Gould plays
the third movement — Rondo — from Beethoven's
Second Piano Concerto.

Each Gould narrative has its own location. The kid genius is always associated with the cottage, the brilliant piano whiz kid with New York, a city he came to loathe. But Gould the media star will also be associated with the Canadian Broadcasting Corporation.

Gould grew up as the CBC grew up, a factor perhaps encouraging in him a greater sense of belonging to the broadcaster. Canada first gave licences for private radio stations in 1922, only to see many of the stations simply rebroadcast American content. The Canadian Broadcasting Corporation was founded in 1936 and mandated to develop programming that was distinctly Canadian, a process accelerated in 1943 with the hiring of Andrew Allan as its new Supervisor of Drama.

Drama? Theatre? This while the Corporation had drama enough as part of its Second World War duties of reporting from the front and producing "plucky-us" documentaries?

A Scottish-born actor, director, and sometime radio announcer, Allan could best be described as something of a practical dandy, a charmer at cocktail parties, stylish, urbane, and a good drinker, but with a quiet resolve to make things happen the way he felt they should happen.

He'd already cultivated connections in New York and London, and was close to major Broadway stars such as Judith Evelyn, formerly of Winnipeg and Hollywood. But in following the CBC brass's wishes to create "definitive" Canadian drama, Allan determinedly surrounded himself with a circle of Canadian writers who would go on to shape the CBC and Canadian culture for decades to come. Fletcher Markle, for one, remained a familiar name to anyone listening to the CBC for the thirty or so years after his *29:40* was first aired on January 23, 1944. This "dramatic essay" by Markle — in fact a radio play about being a radio play — initiated Allan's *Stage 44*, the radio drama series that was to last twelve years, deep into the TV era. Then there was the polymath Lister Sinclair, and Len Peterson, whose prolific and provocative drama for *Stage 44*, *They're All Afraid*, rankled CBC brass no end with its gloomy contradiction of the CBC's aggressively affirmative approach to depicting Canada at war. (The row following the broad-casting of another Peterson play, *The Man with a Bucket of Ashes*, came close to getting Allan sacked.)

Allan later wrote in his autobiography: "My idea of being 'defin-itive' (which I had been told it must be) was to give writers their head, to let them write what they wanted and in the way they wanted to write it. The subtitle on the early *Stages* was a 'report of the state of radio writing in Canada.'"

However much Ottawa's bureaucrats messed around with it, the CBC always managed to incubate great talent. In recent decades much of that talent — say, Lorne Michaels, who created NBC's *Saturday Night Live* from ideas begun and actors met at CBC — has found little future there. Those in Allan's generation — which includes the actor Frank Willis, writers W.O. Mitchell and Harry J. Boyle, and composer Lucio Agostini — became familiar names to Canadians beyond their CBC work and well into the seventies and eighties.

Years later, when talking to John Jessop for *The Canadian Music Book* (1971), Gould said that the *Sunday Night Stage* broadcasts were likely the springboard for his own approach to radio. "I was fascinated with radio. A lot of that kind of ostensibly theatrical radio was also, in a very good sense, documentary making of a rather high order. At any rate, the dis-tinctions between drama and documentary were quite often, it seemed to me, happily and successfully set aside." Toronto's theatre scene wasn't particularly abundant, he added, "and being of sufficiently puritan tem-perament to be disinclined to theatre, even if there had been much of it, I was fascinated with radio theatre because it seemed to me somehow more pure, more abstract, and, in a certain sense, it had a reality for me that, later on, when I became familiar with conventional theatre, that kind of theatre always seemed to lack." He continues: "In the late fifties, I began to write scripts for documentaries occasionally: and I was always dissatisfied with the kind of documentaries that radio seemed to decree. You know, they very often came out sounding — not square, because that's not necessarily a pejorative word in my vocabulary, but they came out sounding — okay, I'll borrow Marshall McLuhan's term — *linear*.

They came out sounding, 'Over to you, now back to our host, and here for the wrap up is' — in a word, predicable."

Gould follows through with this thought, elsewhere, in his "*The Idea of North*: An Introduction," writing: "… *North*, which, though technically a documentary, is at the very least a documentary which thinks of itself as a drama."

Gould's early radio work — and eventually his radio and TV work — was ubiquitous in Canada to the point where many Canadians might well have believed that broadcasting represented his real career, particularly if they were unable to see him live in concert. In fact, piano playing was Gould's reality. Broadcasting was his desire. Before he made his debut recording in 1953 (on Hallmark, a small boutique Toronto recording outfit), Gould had appeared on CBC Radio's *Sunday Morning Recital* on December 4, 1950, playing Mozart and Hindemith sonatas. The acetate tape of the performance given to him as a souvenir of the occasion became a memento he'd retrieve over the years from a shelf in his apartment to remember "that moment in my life when I first had a vague impression of the direction it would take." He increasingly became a fixture at the CBC, with at least two recordings in 1951 and four more in 1952 — one featuring work by Alban Berg and Arnold Schoenberg — the same year he made his high-profile TV debut (on September 8), one of the select performers invited to celebrate the on-air opening of CBLT, the CBC's Toronto station.

A good many tapes in the CBC archives are without dates. One recording in 1953 — one there's a annotation for, that is — is followed by five more in 1954, three as part of the Distinguished Artist Series, then three more in 1955, and so on through the following years, the programs leaning to Bach keyboard work and Beethoven concertos. One CBC archivist told me years ago that there are "probably others things lurking out there, tapes without his name on, we don't know of."

Gould's concert career was heating up over the same period, increasing from fourteen performances in 1955 to twenty-three in 1956 and thirty-six in 1957 to the peak of sixty-five concerts in 1958. His pill-popping kept pace with his gruelling schedule throughout, as did his panic attacks, concert cancellations, complaints about playing conditions, and general distaste for being a tourist. "You begin to feel your age," he told an interviewer. He was only twenty-six years old at the time.

What got him through the night, so to speak, was imagining broadcasting potential and media. This was not a particularly long leap of the imagination in Toronto at the time, what with word spreading rapidly about Marshall McLuhan's communication seminars at the University of Toronto, which were to lead to the formation of the Centre for Culture and Technology in 1963. By then McLuhan seemed to be everywhere. His book *The Mechanical Bride*, which appeared in 1951, explored the emergence of new cultural industries like advertising designed "to get inside the collective public mind." Edmund Carpenter and Harold Innis were, along with McLuhan, the emerging generation of media-mavens centred on the journal *Explorations*, which went a long way to put the U of T and Toronto itself on the international map. "The intellectual excitement of endless dialogue between McLuhan and Carpenter had crystallized into a tangible project with

With Yehudi Menuhin rehearsing for *Duo*, 1966 CBC TV special.

their success in obtaining a grant from the Ford Foundation," writes Canadian historian W. Terrence Gordon in *Marshall McLuhan: Escape into Understanding: A Biography*. It was the foundation's first investment in Canadian culture, U of T president Sidney Smith told McLuhan in a letter.

Indeed. It was an extraordinarily heady time in Toronto, with a flourishing literary scene, artistic collectives such as Painters Eleven, and a flood of new composers in from Europe, such as Oskar Morawetz, putting Canadian composition "at the cross-roads," as Gould recognized at the time. The possibility of being part of such an overlay of media and art production, of controlling it to some degree, of being controlled by it, or a bit of both — and maybe the buzz that comes with the hair-raising sexiness of it all — contributes to the sense of pleasure exuded by most of Gould's TV appearances.

April 13, 1956: Opening Video

GRAPHIC: *People of the moment against the background of their lives*

JOE MCCULLEY: And now, another guest with decided views. A pianist ... Glenn Gould, who, at the age of fourteen, made a solo appearance with the Toronto Symphony Orchestra. Now twenty-three, he's just received international acclaim on the release of a single recording ... Bach's *Goldberg Variations*. Many critics have referred to him as the most astonishing and promising young pianist on the continent.

MUSIC ENDS

MCCULLEY: Good evening, Glenn.

GOULD: Good evening, Mr. McCulley.

MCCULLEY: What were you playing just now?

GOULD: [Tells him and explains that he's rehearsing it for a new recording in New York.]

MCCULLEY: Glenn, in the last few months you've received a lot of attention in *Life* magazine and various other publications. What are your comments about all this publicity?

GOULD: [Replies that he finds it flattering; also that he is glad to say he was first noticed in his own country. Mentions the overplaying of his eccentricities by the press.]

MCCULLEY: What eccentricities, Glenn?

GOULD: [Mentions his need to stay warm and his precautions against cold studios.]

MCCULLEY: Following the success of the *Goldberg Variations* recordings, what have you done apart from your concert work?

GOULD: [Replies he has written a quartet to be performed at Stratford, his future as a composer, etc.]

Gould never looked happier than in the interviews he gave CBC producer Franz Kraemer in 1959 for *Glenn Gould: Off the Record* and *Glenn Gould: On the Record*. The settings for each were to his liking, particularly his family's Uptergrove cottage, with his beloved Chickering piano close at hand, which allowed him to turn around dramatically and play a sparkling atonal passage to prove a point. The many water and landscape shots in the cottage sequences are used to underline Gould's need to get away. But this was cottage country, with boats buzzing by and city executives rushing up on Friday afternoons for the first Scotch, neat. Gould was connected with the city as much as ever.

The other setting for Kraemer's interviews was the famous Steinway basement on West 57th Street in New York City (sadly, gutted in 2014 for condos to be built overhead), where Gould is shown choosing just the right Steinway while surrounded by company men. Steinway, having dealt with the great figures of piano playing over the years, remains famously autocratic in deciding whom to loan their brand-name instruments to. If you're a Steinway star you don't play another brand, as a good many top-flight soloists have found to their consternation. Even Artur Schnabel, the great Beethoven specialist and primarily a player of Bechstein pianos while concertizing in Europe, had to grovel in order for Steinway to allow him out on tour with one of its pianos. But in the latter part of the 1950s, Gould was the dark star of classical music, and the Steinway honchos watched him dart from keyboard to keyboard the way thoroughbred horsemen view a frisky, promising colt.

An entirely more reflective Gould appears on *At Home with Glenn Gould*, with Vincent Tovell, broadcast in 1959. Modelled somewhat on CBS's *Person to Person*, the celebrity interview TV show hosted initially in 1953 by Edward R. Murrow, *At Home* — easily accessed on YouTube — reveals a Gould with gravitas, his "days of glory" as a young teenager long gone. Not yet thirty, he's already wearied by his concert schedule the year before and not looking forward to the upcoming tour, although he admits his schedule — fifty-five or sixty-five performances a year — is modest compared to the hundred-plus performances given yearly by the great pianists of the past. In all, Gould gave some two hundred concerts.

Tovell, quietly calm and authoritative, was the perfect foil for Gould, who could not wait to expound knowledgeably (Russians generally feared playing Bach, and so on). Like Kraemer, Tovell felt he had an intimate understanding of the pianist and thought that he might respond to criticism. Gould biographer Kevin Bazzana says Gould chilled on Tovell after the director made cuts in *Anthology of Variation*, which Tovell and Gould filmed in 1964. At the time, Tovell told Gould cuts were required in his verbose scripts. While prolixity was his style, Gould nevertheless agreed to some cuts, but eventually "terminated the relationship" with Tovell, says Bazzana. But did he? A little later, Cornelia Foss, being wooed by Gould and ready to leave her composer husband Lukas Foss, began signing Tovell's name as a way of covering her tracks. Cornelia Foss became "K. Tovell" or "K. Torell."

Among the many radio interviews Gould gave during the late fifties and early 1960, one of the most important came when he was interviewed in late 1959 (a date disputed in some accounts) by Alan Rich, music director of KPFA in Berkeley, California. Before getting to the *Goldberg*

Variations — still Gould's calling card — Rich drew Gould out about his star status and how he estimated its advantage. "Immense," came Gould's quick reply, not that he had much to do with cultivating this status. He'd never had a publicity person, he pointed out. But, he noted, the media in North America demanded an exaggeration of image. It's "helped build up a certain amount of box office."

Gould foreshadowed much of his later radio work with *Arnold Schoenberg: The Man Who Changed Music* (August 8, 1962), his earliest foray into radio documentary, in which he discussed the pros and cons of the atonal master. The response to the program was mostly positive: Gould had established himself as a Schoenberg expert in theory and practice. However, Gould felt the piece conformed too closely to the stereotypical "now-back-to-our-host" documentary. His dissatisfaction with the program led him to rethink the formal potentials of radio documentary. A direct result was the more dramatically structured and less chatty *Schoenberg: The First Hundred Years*, commissioned by the CBC's John P.L. Roberts for Schoenberg's centenary in 1974. By this time, though, Gould had become more than a radio star — he was more of a radio visionary. The first two segments of *The Solitude Trilogy* — *The Idea of North* in 1967 and *The Latecomers* in 1969, about Newfoundland — made the phrase "contrapuntal radio" (Gould's own description of his documentary-making process) part of just about any discussion of Gould. *Quiet in the Land*, the third part of the radio documentary series, broadcast in 1977, was Gould's favourite.

Gould interviewed a number of people for all three programs, but with the original context altered to suggest a group conversation where none had existed, juxtaposed against train sounds or waves beating against a shore. No wonder Gould billed himself as "writer." In the series Gould channelled his early memories of Andrew Allan's radio theatre and the exhilarating criss-crossing of the line between fact and fiction. In fact, layering or intertwining voices — or relocating them away from the original context — are all ideas as old in music as opera itself; all were prevalent in radio production going back to the 1930s. In Gould's time they were tropes favoured by such new wave Hollywood directors as Robert Altman. Do we bother to mention Sergei Eisenstein's considerable writing on montage, or verbal time compression? Never mind, Gould — having stoically come to terms with his truncated career as a composer of music — was moving ever closer to fulfilling his belief in modern technology's ability to embrace the total musical artwork. Indeed, with "radio-as-music" Gould felt he had rediscovered his compositional touch. Critics agreed. "As a musical work, *North* is a milestone for Gould in developing his compositional voice," was one opinion.

Gould's media sense was refined further with his time at the CBC, where despite his daunting recording schedule — six new releases in 1972 alone — he was able to create a character called Glenn Gould. Nowhere is that more in evidence than in an obscure radio show called "Sports Report," a radio essay recorded in 1972 for *The Scene*, a Saturday morning CBC show produced out of the Corp's old studios on Jarvis Street. *The Scene* rarely rates a word in the writings about Glenn Gould, and then only because of an interview he gave on the show earlier in 1972 about his soundtrack for director George Roy Hill's film *Slaughterhouse-Five*, based on the absurdist Kurt Vonnegut Jr. novel. "Sports Report" is noted in Otto Friedrich's early biography, *Glenn Gould: A Life and Variations*, only as an end-of-book entry in the catalogue prepared by Nancy Canning that outlines all of Gould's TV and radio oeuvre. In Kevin Bazzana's *Wondrous Strange: The Life and Art of Glenn Gould* — pretty much accepted as the most definitive of Gould bios — the show is touched on in one section. There's good reason for this. "Sports Report" seems to have come out of nowhere, a one-off Gould tossed out. Moreover, "Sports Report" is one of the rarest of rare Gould productions in which he doesn't rely for support on his usual music props — musical interludes, musical samples proving a point, snappy set-ups to introduce a point. Yet the show pulls back the curtain on Gould's skillful media manipulation, reflecting his complex motives and role-playing needs. In what is at once a homage to the CBC and a parody of it, he creates a starring role for himself as Glenn Gould while seemingly distancing himself from such a character by having his creations, his multiples, his puppets, his cast of characters all stand in for Gould himself, their creator and string puller. It is Gould playing Gould, but standing at a distance from his self-creation, a distance "that generated the otherness that to him was essential," says Montreal academic Georges

Leroux, in *Partita for Glenn Gould* (translated by Donald Winkler). The performer Gould allowed insight into the performed Gould that he never allowed into his real life.

Gould was a past master at disguising his true feelings. In private, this role-playing seemed to those closest to him a defence mechanism. "If you knew him well, he could take criticism, but you had to be careful," John P.L. Roberts, Gould's mentor at the CBC, once remarked. "He would go into voices of his fictional characters so it really wasn't him you were criticizing."

In keeping with *The Scene*'s usual format, Gould's sports show opens with an attention-grabbing musical sting — in this case, from Bach's Prelude and Fugue No. 10 from *The Well-Tempered Clavier, Vol. 2* — followed by the sound of cheering, then, according to the directions in

Gould's altered ego #1: Karlheinz Klopweisser, avant-gardist.

Gould's altered ego #2: Sir Nigel Twitt-Thornwaite, stuffed-shirt British conductor.

Gould's script, a "hard cut to Moscow announcer in final seconds of the last game of the Canada-Russia series. Slow fade on background and super announcer's intro."

"And that's the way it ended," says Harry Brown, the announcer, describing Team Canada's one-goal victory over the Soviet Union. This, Brown goes on reading from the scriptwriter Gould, is sure to lead to "a re-evaluation by the hockey moguls of the Western World of the intricate, anti-individualistic play-making of the Russian teams."

A wry Newfoundlander, Brown had hosted *As It Happens*, the CBC's ground-breaking evening news show. And Brown understood Gould. Some CBC announcers were utterly baffled by Gould's ornate prose. Not Harry. He had a funny bone. He understood Gould's penchant for self-parody. Whatever games the genius was up to, Harry Brown would play along, too.

THE SPORTING LIFEY

> **BROWN:** Another result … has been the decision by the production responsible for *The Scene* to commission the following comments on the game from Glenn Gould.
>
> **GOULD:** Thank you, Harry.
>
> Brown: But allow me to read that last line again with appropriate italics … to commission the following comments on the games from — *GLENN GOULD!!!*
>
> [That's how Gould's script reads, complete with this name in italics followed by the three hammer blow exclamation marks. Brown's voice, however, clearly means to suggest a question mark, as if saying, "If you can believe it."]
>
> **GOULD:** Do you presume to question my competence in the field, sir?
>
> **BROWN:** In the field, perhaps not, but, in the gondola, as Foster Hewitt would say, I most certainly do.
>
> **GOULD:** May I remind you, sir, that no red-blooded Canadian boy can be oblivious to the high stakes devolving upon the Russia-Canada confrontation.
>
> **BROWN:** No, that's quite true, but since you're, presumably, not just here to ice the puck, as we say at penalty-killing time, I can only assume, Glenn, that you're about to fire a slap-shot at some particular goal of your own.

GOULD: That I am, Harry.

BROWN: Well, why don't we have a face-off then, and see who gets control of the puck.

GOULD: Fair enough!! Actually, I do have a particular angle that I want to play —

BROWN: … which I, as the opposition goalie will, of course, attempt to cut off.

GOULD: Okay. But I've got to warn you that from long years of practising glissandi, I've got a mean back-hand. So watch out for the rebound!

And off we go, carried along by the genial back-and-forth of civilized radio broadcasting entering its twilight years in the shadow of the confrontational and embittered talk radio that was emerging. We were all radioheads in the early seventies, but for most of us radio meant FM radio, where we got the chance to hear the longest cuts on the album. For Glenn Gould, radio meant the CBC, its tone and rhythms deep in his memory from listening to the network as a kid. It was his "wallpaper," as he called it. The CBC was another sanctuary, another creative techno man-cave with its home-for-the-holidays glow of lights and dials.

BROWN: Well, may I suggest that before you get any further off-side and we run out of double-entendres that you get to the point.

GOULD: Well, I would, but my left-winger isn't paying attention.

BROWN: [in mock despair] Will it never end?

GOULD: Okay, I'll stop ragging the puck and get down to business. You're quite right, Harry, I do have an angle. I'm opposed to competitive sport and I …

BROWN: To all competitive sport?

GOULD: Practically all of it. Yes.

Coming across the show in the radio archives at CBC headquarters in Toronto, I was reminded that I'd worked on *The Scene* as a freelance editor/producer in the early 1970s, although I wasn't involved in either of Gould's appearances on the show.

"Sports Report" has a deceptive casualness to it, as the script wanders from idea to idea, each with a Gould-created character — a boxer, a radio producer, a psychiatrist, and an explorer — as a mouthpiece, every one of them circling the single premise: Glenn Gould's aversion to conflict. It's a radio newshour version of a theme and variations but in reverse, with variations coming before the theme. It's Glenn Gould as theme and his many characters as variations of Glenn Gould all having a marvellous time of it.

"I'm absolutely convinced, despite the old saw about the fact that a good novelist is someone who does not need a nom de plume, that a certain part of your persona operates efficiently within the structure of a certain life style, a certain name," he told journalist Jonathan Cott, in *Conversations with Glenn Gould*. "I, for instance, was incapable of writing in a sustained humorous style until I developed an ability to portray myself pseudonymously," channelling Herbert von Karajan for his own "Herbert von Hochmeister."

"Once I did that," Gould went on, "I found it no problem at all to say what I wanted to say in a humorous style. Until then, there was a degree of inhibition that prevented me from doing so. But then the floodgates were open, and subsequently I developed a character for every season."

Without mentioning him directly, Gould appears to be thinking about Oscar Wilde and his feeling that "man is least himself when he talks in his own person."

"Give him a mask," Wilde went on, "and he will tell you the truth."

Gould continued: "I am fascinated with the fact that most of our value judgments relate to an awareness of identity: we tend to be terribly frightened of making judgments if we're not aware of the identity of whoever is responsible for a piece of art. And I am fascinated with that idea — in fact the most joyous moments in radio, as opposed to my most creative ones, perhaps are those when I can turn to impersonation."

The CBC was fertile ground for this kind of thinking, having a cast of characters uniquely its own, most famously Charlie Farquharson, writer/actor Don Harron's savvy cornball rube, and Rawhide, announcer Max Ferguson's … cornball savvy rube. Gould understood the fine line between reality and fiction walked by Charlie and Rawhide, how they both sounded like people everyone knew. (Harron and Ferguson, who both knew Gould, had finely tuned ears to regional accents, almost a must considering the CBC's far-flung listenership.) One of the characters Gould drew on the most was Teddy ("It ain't subtle") Slutz, the archetypal New York cabbie who with his "yah know what I mean" attitude was modelled on a real New York cabbie who gave Gould a ride from Columbia's 33rd Street studio to his hotel. But an even busier character in the Gould radio of the mind was, well, Glenn Gould, CBC highbrow homeboy and resident musical genius. It was a good time in the late sixties and early seventies to reinvent oneself, as the CBC was in the process of reinventing itself, creating a roster of new stars that included David Suzuki, Barbara Frum, and Peter Gzowski.

"Sports Report" manipulates our basic understanding of what we're hearing by playing with our perception of radio content and format; Gould based it on the phone interview format used to great effect on CBC Radio's influential news show *As It Happens*. This bending and blurring of barriers between drama and documentary, between the real and the fictional, was something Gould had found absolutely magical when listening to CBC drama where "the distinctions between drama and documentary were quite often, it seemed to me, happily and successfully set aside," as he said.

"The fact that there is presumably some kernel of news underlying your process is an excuse," he told John Jessop in the piece *Radio as Music*. "It's the most glorious of excuses really and it sets you free, first of all, to deal with art in the factual, assured way in which one customarily deals with pure information. At the same time it permits you to transform that information into what in the olden days one would have referred to as 'works of art.'"

Gould scholars point to the stacks of yellow legal notepads he kept close at hand as the best source for understanding Gould's inner life. And, yes, the notes can make for rather harrowing reading when they list his increasing physical woes. "Constant adjustment re: back," he scribbles at one point. Yet the notepads are curiously unrevealing, for the most part, for one who loved writing as Gould did, as if he consciously avoided including in them anything really deeply felt or introspective or revealing. It's best to take them as notes helping shape the formation of official Gould policy on anything and everything, even if that means the shaping of a love note or an intimate letter to his father, Bert.

Threading its way through "Sports Report" is another emotion, one Gould dreaded yet could barely hide: anger. Behind the program's genial banter there bristles a righteous anger that might be found in any barn-burner of a Sunday sermon in many a Southern Ontario church. Gould doesn't quite call competition a "sin," but that's what he means. Brown (i.e., Gould) wonders rhetorically if Gould is equating "an almost sedentary, certainly intellectual pastime like chess" with "a championship fight."

> GOULD: I certainly am. May I recall for you the
> immortal words of one Bobby Fischer, and I quote, "I
> like to see them squirm. I want to crush their egos."
>
> BROWN: Hmm.

Fischer was in the news, having defeated Boris Spassky in the famous "Cold War of chess" in Reykjavik, Iceland, played from July 11 to August 31, 1972. It was attended by Harold C. Schonberg, the *New York Times* music critic, sometime Gould critic, and chess buff who, awestruck by Fischer, had already called him "the Mozart of chess." Following Fischer's decisive victory after the twenty-one matches, he became the "Beethoven of Chess" in Schonberg's eyes.

> GOULD: I'm surprised he didn't manage to dub
> Spassky the Cherubini of Chess or the Salieri of Chess
> or something while he was at it.
>
> BROWN: [Laughs]
>
> GOULD: But, anyway, he decided to upgrade Fischer
> because he claimed to have discovered qualities of
> Beethoven-like innovation in Fischer's variational play.

BROWN: And I dare say a certain amount of egomania played its part in the parallel.

Gould had an ambivalent attitude toward Schonberg, who, among others things, once suggested Gould "plays things slow" because "maybe his technique is not so good," and further mused that perhaps the Canadian upstart wasn't quite professional enough to make it in a big-time musical centre like New York. Here, however, Gould is struck by a piece Schonberg wrote for the *New York Times* titled "Psychic Murder at the Chess Board."

Gould's own fascination with Fischer might also have been rooted in his recognition of a fellow genius/obsessive/recluse who commanded the world's attention with the enormity of his talent. Others who've followed Gould certainly saw parallels. In his memoir, *Parallel Play: Growing Up with Undiagnosed Asperger's,* Tim Page — editor of *The Glenn Gould Reader* — explains how he came to see Fischer and Gould as role models along with Howard Hughes and J.D. Salinger, each one of them a recluse. Liz Garbus's documentary *Bobby Fischer Against the World* sparked reviews that commented on the Gould/Fischer parallels, among them their willingness to abandon centre stage at the peak of their powers. Gould, who could end friendships abruptly without a word, thought that Fischer's ruthlessness toward his opponents was as potentially harmful as the "more easily quantifiable danger of a prize fight."

BROWN: Am I to assume then that you see the competitiveness of sport as a metaphor for other types of competition" ["in life," was added in the original script], as well?

GOULD: Absolutely. And that is precisely the point I want to pursue.

BROWN: Well, before you pursue it, may I play you a brief interview that I taped earlier this week?

GOULD: Of course.

BROWN: Well then, when I heard you were going to talk about sports, etc., I had the sneaking suspicion that you would hold forth rather negatively on the subject.

And so we are introduced first to Dominico Pastrano, "up-and-coming young Canadian welterweight." In the early 1970s, the fight game was having a golden age, arguably its last, with the lightweight Roberto Durán and heavyweight greats Muhammad Ali and Joe Frazier. Even more salient for Gould, Durán, Ali, and many others in this generation of boxers were media savvy, using nonstop, intrusive media attention to layer and nuance their developing personas. Gould knew a character like Dominico Pastrano would play well with a CBC audience in tune with the broad comic parodies and send-ups of Wayne and Shuster.

BROWN: [to Dominico, aka Glenn Gould] I guess I should congratulate you, first of all, because I understand that, according to *Ring Magazine*, you're now ranked No. 9 in the world in your division.

PASTRANO (GOULD): Geez, Mac, you must be reading some real out-of-date issues, you know, 'cause, like right now I'm listed as No. 7 and ah —"

Pastrano is the Brooklynite-sounding cousin of Theodore Slutz, who alone among Gould's pantheon of stand-ins and doppelgängers was allowed to be Gould's chief music critic. Pastrano's musings about the politics of boxing ("it's a pretty political thing, you know, being No. 7 in the world and all that") allowed Gould to take a shot at the competition in the classical music business, just as he was taking a poke at competition in general. "Most of the guys that are in front of me — supposedly, that is," says Pastrano, "they don't want to mess with me 'cause they know I'm pretty good and fast and, like, they got a lot to lose, losin' to me, you know." As it turns out, Pastrano's manager is "from the States" and has particular respect for Richard Nixon, wanting his protégé, Dominic, to start thinking more like Nixon. Gould, long fascinated with American politics, simply could not avoid commenting on Nixon, particularly while the president was on a roll. The Watergate scandal, although gaining traction, was still a story for the inside pages of the papers. Tricky Dick still seemed all-powerful on the front page. He completed his signature foreign policy triumph by opening diplomatic relations with China and was en route to re-election in one of the greatest lopsided victories in American presidential politics, trouncing the Democratic challenger George McGovern. "Nixon is like the champ, you know, or maybe, considering the Russians and all, he might be the leading contender," says Pastrano. Guys on top of their form don't dally with lesser talents. Nixon would be "really stupid" to "come out and fight" McGovern, says Pastrano. The president, bruised during four televised confrontations with Kennedy in 1960, not only didn't debate McGovern in 1972, but he rarely mentioned his opponent's name during the campaign.

> **BROWN:** Well, I've often noticed that our leading sports columnists categorize you as a boxer rather than a fighter. In other words, they usually dwell upon the elegance and deftness of your movements in the ring, and, in that regard, you're very frequently compared to Muhammad Ali …
>
> [Pastrano says he's flattered, but Brown has only just begun.]
>
> I've noticed again and again in regard to your style that you have a balletic grace in the ring and I was wondering whether classical ballet has played any part in your life or whether any particular dancers have influenced you?
>
> **PASTRANO:** Well, like, I ain't never gone in for that sort of thing too much, you know. But I remember one time, on *The Ed Sullivan Show*, I think it was, there was a guy — I think he was from Russia named Rudy something or other —
>
> **BROWN:** Rudolf Nureyev, perhaps?

PASTRANO: Yeah, could have been [in an early draft of the script, Gould scratches out "it" before the word "could"], and like, I noticed with him that there was a certain similarity with my style, you know.

BROWN: Well, that's exactly what I was getting at, Dominico.

PASTRANO: Yeah, I mean, first of all, he was really fast, and his reflexes seemed to be okay, you know, and, like, when another, ah, dancer was coming toward him he could give him the clips pretty good. But like the main thing I noticed about his style, you know, is that he kept out of the corners, you know. I mean he was mostly in the centre of the ring … I couldn't help but noticing that he kept out in the centre territory practically all the time, so I was pretty impressed by that, you know.

To anyone who would not recognize Gould, his voice, or his penchant for giving a character he created his own opinions and feelings, "Sports Report" might have sounded truly odd-ball. *Chess, boxing, and Nureyev all in a matter of minutes?* For Gould, the show reflected his confidence as an established multi-tasking, all-round radio guy: the star commentator, producer, theorist, and familiar character. It reflected his sense of belonging, particularly with all its infra-dig CBC Radio references.

To anyone who spent any time with them, Gould's fictional creations seemed to have been arranged in hierarchical order according to his need for them. Those most extravagantly un-Gould-like were, like Pastrano the boxer or Slutz the cabbie, allowed to spill the beans on real Gould feelings. In this way, Gould left a silent warning: believe this if you dare, you smug intellectuals. Characters sounding most like him — sounding the way Gould himself does while playing one of his fictions — acted as spokesmen for the ideas crossing his radar. His character John Greeves, *The Scene's* next interview, reflects Gould's early-seventies multi-tasking CBC self.

Greeves — a thinly disguised version of CBC producer John McGreevy — is, like Gould, prodigiously talented on more than one front. Greeves was a recognized media powerhouse and name-dropping BBC producer, mentioning the likes of "Sir Kenneth, an absolute brick." (Kenneth Clark's thirteen-week *Civilisation* series had recently made the ultra-patrician Clark a transatlantic celebrity.) Yet Greeves is additionally a world-class Olympic track star with thoughts about testing the limits of human capability. Greeves's "dazzling 26-week series, *Civilization of the Newt*" (fictional, of course), is based on the work of Czech writer Karel Čapek (*War with the Newts* was the title of Čapek's novel; his play, *R.U.R.*, for Rossum's Universal Robots, introduced the word *robot*). Greeves doesn't linger long on sci-fi as Gould edits away any further delving into it. Nonetheless, elements of sci-fi — its quasi-religious nature, its smooth techno surface — hover over Gould's work, as does the work of authors such as Čapek and Kafka. (Composer R. Murray Schafer remembers arguing with Gould when both were students over the merits of Kafka and Thomas Mann, with Gould preferring Kafka.)

> **FACTORY MANAGER HARRY DOMIN:** Young Rossum invented a worker with the minimum amount of requirements. He had to simplify him. He rejected everything that did not contribute directly to the progress of work. He rejected everything that makes man more expensive. In fact, he rejected man and made the Robot. My dear Miss Glory, the Robots are not people. Mechanically they are more perfect than we are, they have an enormously developed intelligence, but they have no soul. Have you ever seen what a Robot looks like inside?
>
> **HUMANITY LEAGUE PRESIDENT HELENA GLORY:** Good gracious, no!
>
> **DOMIN:** Very neat, very simple. Really a beautiful piece of work.

It's not hard to link Gould and sci-fi, even if he didn't himself. I came across *Wyrm*, a future fantasy by American psychiatrist and sci-fi author

Mark Fabi that appeared in 1998 and zeroes in on a computer-created role-playing game that portends world destruction. In one scene, the main figures in the story begin listening to a CD of Gould's *Goldberg* at George's place.

"George likes Bach because he thinks if he were still alive today, he'd be a hacker."

"Not would-be. Bach was a hacker. He just programmed for organs and harpsichords and stuff. What's a musical score anyway? It's an algorithm."

"Sports Report" evolved to be its own algorithm, answering questions only it asks, a set of variations flowing in varying directions yet bound by original design to evolve from a single, simple theme, a process of almost robotic orderliness.

"One tends to become hypnotized by one's metaphoric conceits," Gould has Greeves saying at one point later in the program. It's Gould chastising Gould for being so … *so Gouldian* and not, *gad sir,* wanting it any other way. "That's the problem with art, really," he continues. "It takes such very indirect routes to achieve ordinary destinations. I think this is because we stopped believing in magic years back; well, perhaps the younger chaps have come back to it — but for my generation, I'm afraid the transcendence of the spirit was a phenomenon more talked about than felt, and in a sense symbolic logic, thanks to Mr. Freud and his friends, became our substitute for magic, and we tried, some of us quite desperately, to believe in it …"

But there's magic in the air. Greeves/Gould mulls a moment or two before admitting that there's a "chance (the original script had the word as *change*) for magic to enter in. You see, there's always the possibility that some mysterious magnetic field will stop all the clocks just for one precious moment, defy all the laws of gravity and probability, and, as it does so, pull us inexorably toward it — the zero minute mile."

The wistfulness here is extraordinary, and through it one cannot but remember the final sentence in *The Great Gatsby:* "So we beat on, boats against the current, borne back ceaselessly into the past."

Listeners to "Sports Report" would by now have reason to believe that the subject of sport had long stopped providing any direction for them to follow. Gould was now appearing as Dr. Wolfgang von Krankmeister, a psychiatrist who comments rather disparagingly about the character of the two previous guests. Gould's other shrink was S.F. Lemming, M.D., a swipe at Peter F. Ostwald, a psychiatrist and Gould biographer who met the pianist in San Francisco but was dropped by Gould in the late seventies.

"Is there a Bible at the CBC?" von Krankmeister asks.

"Yes," answers Harry Brown. "The Gideon Society provides one for each of the announcer booths."

"It's one thing to say that an artist describes in his work the way things are with the world," Gould says, now in his voice, as Glenn Gould; "it's quite another when he has no alternative precisely because that's the way things are with him."

Duncan Haig Guinness, the last character on Gould's imaginary roundtable, is a CBC producer located among the musk oxen somewhere in Gould's mythic Arctic paradise. His appearance becomes a disappearance, as the imaginary phone line connecting them for the imaginary interview mysteriously goes dead.

"This is a recording," says the imaginary operator. "The number you have reached is not a working number. Please consult your directory for further information."

FINIS

"The musical genius is a nut,"
by Duncan Macpherson.

CHAPTER THREE

The "Con"

JACK

Dad parked the ten-year-old maroon Chevy near the Bathurst Street Bridge and we walked over to the rusted-out railing. Trains clanked by underneath, but the stop we were making wasn't only about them. We were looking down on the hunkered-down city that lay to the east of our only regular stop on the way to my piano lesson at the Royal Conservatory of Music downtown.

Toronto itself wasn't much of a lure. It wasn't a "big city" in any sense of *big* that a teenager might care for. Nor was it tall; tall was exciting. Real skyscrapers — rumoured to be found all over New York — were something out of the comics. Spiderman swung from one to the other. Superman was able to leap over them. But Toronto? Toronto was squat. Toronto was serious. And so was everything in it.

Nothing about the city seemed more high-minded and serious to outsiders than the Royal Conservatory of Music. My father, Jack, called it the "Con," with no double entendre intended — he taught there for years. A lot of parents loved the word *royal* being attached to the school their kid was attending, a significant upgrade from the days when it was called the Toronto Conservatory of Music.

Ken Phillips's drawing of the Royal Conservatory's lilac garden on University Avenue with its cast-iron fence.

It was there I met Miss Butler, a large, soft woman in a billowy purple dress that left her as shapeless as a cumulus cloud. Her pale skin received further lightening from a dusting of talc. I wouldn't dream of pretending to know or daring to say her first name — it was "Margaret" — at the time. She terrified me. She taught me to listen, though. The clarity of touch and thinking demanded by Miss Butler for Debussy is fixed forever in my head. ("Hear the tintinnabulations of the bells as you play," she'd say as I was beginning Debussy's *La Cathédrale engloutie*, making each "t" in tintinnabulation sound as crisp as a communion wafer.)

The Con, at the southwest corner of University Avenue and College Street and bordering the University of Toronto, was more than half a century old when my dad began to teach there in the 1940s. Approached from College Street, the Con's façade gave the impression that no line ran exactly parallel to any other line. Seen from behind — looking north as you made your way up University Avenue — the Con became a hodge-podge of smaller attached structures, residences mostly for out-of-town students, male and female, "single room $420 to $460" per year. Each sub-building connected to another annex and to the main building and, on occasion, to the ground itself, by a bewildering iron latticework of fire escapes. I don't know if any lives were saved, but maybe a certain number of individuals can thank their lives' start to those fire escapes. Men were forbidden in the rooms at most times, and young lady students had to be in by eleven at night or there'd be hell to pay. Ah, but those fire escapes allowed for plenty of rule-breaking and sneaking up and out and down. Harry Freedman, the Canadian composer and oboist and a very hand-some guy, by his own report was particularly agile.

The Conservatory was a place where doors opened up on who knew what, maybe a closet or a studio or a space with *another* door on the other side. It was a place with stairs that led who knew where. Down and up were only two of several possibilities. The halls themselves were weird in the horror movie way halls can be called weird. "They squeaked," singer Robert Goulet remembered when I talked to him decades later. "Loudly. Very loudly. It was as if the halls had some life form under them. They always squeaked, whether you walked or ran. They squeaked."

The Con was sometimes a set and sometimes a stage, one folded around the other in one place. In either case, everyone stayed in char-acter. The opera coach, Dr. Ernesto Vinci — a German Jew born Ernst Moritz who was once mentored by Toscanini — would seemingly float down the main hall from his third-floor aerie, where he taught voice, sur-rounded on every side by the fluttering of sopranos and mezzos, talking all at once to him, to each other, giggling, laughing, their impromptu trills pinging off the hall walls, their makeup on high alert. There was the parade in the basement cafeteria where, with lunch as a side order, the egos and reputations of those not in attendance were fried, broiled, or roasted, all done to suit the crowd's taste. As Lois Marshall remem-bered, "Everybody gathered to take things apart and put things back together again." The cafeteria, thankfully, was cheap, with good food. I remember Gould and R. Murray Schafer talking animatedly. Schafer was just getting started, Gould already a superstar. But the cafeteria made everyone equal. Besides, getting fed in those days was not always a cer-tainty. Robert Goulet (not yet a superstar), perennially broke, relied on free coffees from pals in the cafeteria. When they weren't forthcoming he might go entirely without eating, as he told me years later, if the little Hungarian lady running his boarding house didn't give him some goulash now and then.

You learned to tell who played what, which student or which teacher, or who did what by looks alone: the fiddlers, thin to gaunt and with their scarily keen eyes as if they were spying on something; the composers, fusty-looking in shirts, ties, vests, and cardigans, with pockets full of pencils. Pianists came in all shapes and sizes, their appearance telling little of their ability. But Glenn Gould in his time mystified everyone by his age, or rather, lack of it.

The Conservatory had only begun to shake loose from its provincial roots when I studied there in the fifties, a good decade after Gould was there and when, by all accounts, it was a minor British outpost not up to standards set in New York, Berlin, and elsewhere. No wonder Gould would learn to hate the British military character of the contests and exams and develop a life-long loathing of competition of any type. The Conservatory's reception area, with its overstuffed couches and wickets for paying tuition fees, had the aura of a railway station in some provincial English town.

Yet in truth, there was a certain oddball-ness built into it. Think of Harry Potter's Hogwarts with fewer shadows and with streetcars outside, not hippogriffs or whatever those flying lizards are in the film. This wasn't just a building with an inner life. This was a building with an inner life that had gotten out of hand. And this getting out of hand was not likely to stop, given the sag and sway of the building. Old photographs don't show this much. The old place appears to be barely standing upright. But a charcoal sketch by Ken Phillips — a lesser-known Toronto artist with a fine sense of whimsy — gets it right. The Con looked like an old frigate. Given a mast and enough canvas, it could set sail. It did, in a way. Sold to Ontario Hydro in 1962 and then razed, it moved its operations to its new postmodernist digs on Bloor Street.

As a business it was the only game in town, providing Canada-wide exams through staffers such as my father who crossed the country by train twice a year to such far-flung locales as Flin Flon and Moose Jaw. Outside Toronto, such was the Con's elevated reputation that many a small-town paper would see Dad's arrival as worthy of a story, sometimes with picture attached: he would be identified as the Conservatory's "representative," like some distinguished ambassador visiting the far reaches of an empire.

The Conservatory was, as I was reminded time and again, the centre of all things musical in Toronto, and around which circled such moons in lesser orbits as the Kiwanis Music Festival, music competitions at the Canadian National Exhibition and elsewhere, and active music scenes in North York or Weston or Etobicoke, themselves centred on a branch of the RCM. It was, of course, the only place where the young Glenn Gould would go, and Florence enrolled her son in the Conservatory in 1940.

FLORRIE

"I cannot remember when I first commenced to play, for my mother tells me that I wanted to reach out for the keyboard before I was out of her arms. I have also learned that when I was about two and one-half years of age, I could quite readily play after my mother, anything that the size of my hand[s] would permit me to play."

The quote isn't from Glenn Gould, but from Pepito Arriola, the Spanish-born piano virtuoso of the early twentieth century whose violin playing later eclipsed his piano work. Josefa Rodriquez Carballeira, Arriola's mother — his father had skipped town when he was very young — was parading her son's talent before the world before he was six. Same with Rose Grainger, who hustled her son Percy, an Australian-born composer, pianist, and sadomasochism aficionado. Musical fathers — Liszt's or Mozart's, most notably — were no less aggressive when it came to developing their talented offspring. In general, though, the mother often spots the talent first, even in the womb, as was with case with Florence Greig Gould, who cranked up the radio while she was pregnant for the education of the unborn prodigy. Some Gould chroniclers believe it was her humming that encouraged his own.

Florence discovered early on that Glenn had perfect pitch — the ability to hear a note even if unplayed, a gift all right, but not one particularly helpful to a pianist — and an unusual capacity to remember things. While sifting through Gould material in Ottawa I came across Gould's earliest music study books, the kind with the pretty drawings decorating the staves, and I noticed how few marks were in them. Seemingly, Gould saw, absorbed, and played them from this single snapshot of understanding. But Glenn wasn't by his own understanding a child prodigy, even though at six or seven he wanted to practise while other kids were outside playing. And at that tender age he was already in the habit of protecting his hands — *no ball games, please* — and worrying about his health. Florence Gould encouraged him. I've already told how when he was six Glenn was taken to hear Josef Hofmann, the Polish-born American pianist and head of the piano department the Curtis Institute of Music in Philadelphia. The concert left "a staggering impression" on him, he would say later.

I found the aforementioned reminiscence by Arriola in a dusty first edition of *Great Pianists on Piano Playing* (1913), James Francis Cooke's compilation of practical advice gathered from an enormous array of piano talents who, for the most part, have been entirely forgotten today, Arriola among them. So for every Vladimir de Pachmann on "Seeking Originality" and S.V. Rachmaninoff on "Essentials of Artistic Playing," there are essays by Alberto Jonas ("Nervousness in Piano Playing"), Yolanda Mero ("Thoroughness in Hungarian Music Study"), and X. Scharwenka ("Economy in Music Study"). But the profession of professional pianism being addressed by Cooke and company — concerts without end, with occasional radio broadcasts — was by the time Gould arrived on the scene in its twilight years. So Gould more or less invented himself, with guidance from his mentor and teacher Alberto Guerrero. (Although Gould might well have read Alberto Jonas, "Nervousness in Piano Playing," particularly the part that reads: "The musician should also know that the normal cure for nervous conditions is not to be found so much in medicine bottles, as in work accomplished without hurry or flurry but with care and a happy mind, plenty of rest, the right food and the right mental attitude [state of mind].")

Gould's talent was spotted instantly. He started organ lessons in 1942 with Frederick Silvester — "Freddie," my dad always called him, though it was hardly appropriate for such a solemn British gent. Soon he was receiving medals, high marks, and raves from other Con teachers, particularly Healey Willan, the organist and choirmaster, one of the most respected musicians in the city at the time. With all this as further proof of her son's genius, Florence next decided the Conservatory itself wasn't good enough for her son, and in 1943 she managed to have Glenn accepted as a student by Alberto Guerrero, the Chilean-born pianist, the lessons taking place in his own penthouse studio at 51 Grosvenor Street.

Guerrero saw himself as something of an outsider as well, and avoided the Con as much as possible, all the while accepting the best of young players to study at his studio. With its Picasso prints and a wide range of books, Guerrero's studio was more of a salon. It was a lesson in sophistication to those familiar only with the sterile sheen of the Con's hallways, the cigar and cigarette smoke billowing from the teachers' lounge.

The Gould-Guerrero relationship, while clearly of great benefit to Gould, has been the subject of as much speculation as anything else in Guerrero's life and almost anything in Gould's. The two remained close for many years, and Gould visited the Guerrero cottage from time to time. Later, though, Gould did his best to distance himself from his teacher's influence.

Guerrero's musical sophistication certainly lit up Gould's imagination, much the way Guerrero's demanding, professional-level technical approach — the crouched sitting position at the keyboard, the finger strengthening by tapping the playing finger with another, the memory exercises — was absorbed by Gould in his own approach.

Historically, Guerrero's impact on Toronto has been successfully encapsulated in the biography *In Search of Alberto Guerrero*, written by one of his former students, John Beckwith, who chronicled his mentor's life from its Chilean beginnings. Guerrero's reputation at the time is vividly shown by the rates the Conservatory was asking for the services of its "pianoforte staff" for each series of lessons:

$50: Kihl, Viggo; Kolessam, Lubka; Seitz, Ernest
$45: Guerrero, Alberto; Welsman, Frank S.
$40: Berlin, Boris
$20: Kraus, Greta

Talent and potential were measured at the Conservatory by whom you studied with. Progress was measured by the exams you passed as you dutifully mounted the Conservatory grade-book ladder step by step, grade by grade on the way to the giddy heights of Associate status. The exams en route were optional but necessary, if only for the parents, to measure progress and offer proof that family money was well spent. Many of the more devoted (or scared) students took an exam for all even grades: four, six, eight, and ten. In June 1945 Gould passed his exam for the degree of ATCM (Associate of the Toronto Conservatory of Music) with the highest marks in the class.

That fall — he was now thirteen years old and starting grade nine at Malvern Collegiate Institute in Scarborough— he was already described as "the Ten Hottest Fingers." At school? On the street? In town? Soon enough it was all three. On passing his theory exam in 1946 Gould was awarded his Associateship, again at the top of his class.

Some commentary suggests an Associate designation automatically conferred professional status. In most cases — mine included — it didn't. The majority of Associates might be described as skilled amateurs, average citizens with some particular talent for music. In Gould's case, however, it was the last official preparatory hurdle before he headed out into uncharted concert-giving territory. In November 1945, and again in May 1946, Gould played the opening movement of Beethoven's Fourth Piano Concerto, the first time with Guerrero playing the orchestral part, the second time with Conservatory principal Ettore Mazzoleni leading the Conservatory Symphony Orchestra at Massey Hall. On January 14 and 15, 1947, he performed the entire Fourth with the Toronto Symphony led by Sir Bernard Heinze. On October 20 of the same year at the Eaton Auditorium, he made his professional recital debut for International Artists with a fairly standard program (Scarlatti, Beethoven, Chopin), which, however, also included a Couperin *passacaille* arranged by Guerrero. The program was repeated a month later in Toronto. And on December 3 in Hamilton, Ontario, Gould performed Beethoven's Piano Concerto No. 1 with Sir Ernest MacMillan leading the Toronto Symphony.

The young Gould was a story, a local story maybe, at first, but one everyone outside of Toronto music circles was hearing about. Take my

Learning the fiddle.

family. We'd moved from downtown Toronto when I was about six to farm country in Mississauga. Eager, cheery, early suburbanites — imagine Cary Grant and Myrna Loy in the 1948 movie *Mr. Blandings Builds His Dream House* — my parents immediately fashioned my father's music studio out of the still-smelly poured concrete of the basement, even though a ladder was all there was connecting the first floor to the second. He built up a piano class of young kids. My mother made them cookies. I went to school. We settled in. I went weekly to the Conservatory for piano lessons. But for me and my parents, Toronto had disappeared over the horizon, a cloud glow by night but of little consequence except when it came to the annual trip to the Canadian National Exhibition in late August and to Eaton's at Christmastime.

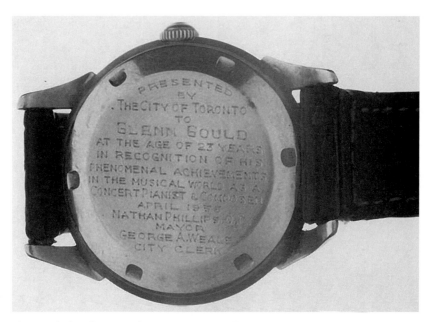

The watch that the City of Toronto gave Gould in 1956.

My father lost contact with his old musical life, except for a few friends. Then he started hearing more and more about this Glenn Gould. *Gould was terrible. Gould was brilliant.* My mother explained to me that Dad felt he needed to hear him, as did all the other piano people they knew, because this Gould was up to something, and piano players, like chess masters, had to keep up on the latest moves. So one April night my parents, who never went anywhere, headed to what was Gould's now-famous 1956 Massey Hall triumph, where he received a watch from the City of Toronto, a testament to the already many years he'd performed in such a commanding manner. To confirm the importance of the night, my mom, Audrey, wore a fur stole — a rare bit of flash for her.

I waited up, but they said little after they got back late that night. Mother put away the fur that was seen next at my brother Michael's wedding many years later. She then went upstairs, leaving Dad and me alone for a moment, not that common for us. Maybe he wanted to talk. Yet when I asked him what he thought about the night — a one-pianist-to-another sort of thing — he seemed distant. Normally, Dad was a capital-*R*

Romantic when it came to music, as a listener, as a teacher, and as a player. So he was prepared to be unsettled by this Glenn Gould. He thought he'd known what to expect: the hijinks, the singing, the Bach beyond brilliant (Gould's debut recording of Bach's *The Goldberg Variations* that year had shaken things up even for those who hadn't heard it).

But there had been something else. After thinking about it, he said: "We all know the pieces he played, or most of them. We've played the same notes and have heard ourselves play them. But he made it seem we'd been playing different things all along."

MONK

A generational thing was at work here. The core set of Gould's prodigious gifts — musicality, technique, memory, serious intent — were well understood in their own way by Gould's professional peers and older teachers: he was part of the tradition, even when he forgot about the dignified part. He was the "next" Horowitz or the "next" someone else. But these were insiders, and their understanding of Gould was being challenged by what was happening all around.

Start with the piano. The piano was sort of the TV of its day, stretching back to the early nineteenth century. Almost every middle-class or affluent household had one: a modest upright in a modest house, the grand for the grand house, but prominently displayed in both. The middle-class longing for culture insisted that daughters — and some sons — learn how to play the damn thing or Father would want an explanation. Conservatories were founded and prospered on this need, as did the makers of pianos, music teachers, and travelling soloists with gilded reputations.

These cozy family connotations of the piano had changed. The instrument was now used every which way for every sort of reason, but less and less as the source of home entertainment. Modernist composers such as Henry Cowell and John Cage were banging on it and plucking its strings, ignoring the keys as they went. The "prepared piano" is what they called the instrument. A new kind of piano star emerged. In the early movies, Chico Marx of the Marx Brothers — who "never practised" and soaked his hands in hot water pre-performance — was reaching audiences unimaginable to Artur Schnabel (and most likely not desired by Schnabel). With early jazz, Earl Hines and Art Tatum displayed technical and emotional range rivalled by only a few of the greatest classical soloists of the day.

Gould seemed a part of all this, part of *all* piano playing, not just classical piano playing; his blistering attack was pure jazz in its intensity, his stage presence pure theatre. And he was reaching a generation that had no qualms about that — my generation, that is, but not my father's.

I first saw Gould after I'd seen Jerry Lee Lewis. By then, the difference between them was purely academic — *Great Bachs of Fire*. I'd also fallen head-over-heels for jazz on my first hearing of Jess Stacy's unplanned piano solo on Benny Goodman's live 1938 performance of "Sing Sing Sing" at Carnegie Hall; here was spontaneity as gorgeously crafted as any Brahms intermezzo. Ray Charles's pounding gospel chords and finger slithering off the black keys got me playing, a Mississauga white boy, in that direction, too. And Gould was part of all that. He helped make Bach part of it.

Jazzers loved Bach. Always had. Gould had trouble with jazz, but not jazz players, and particularly not pianist Bill Evans. The two men talked to each other on a regular basis. Gould got to feel jazz a bit through playing some of Beethoven's most bumptious arpeggiated moments, which felt like swing when they really started rocking. (Canadian pianist Stewart Goodyear can get into the same space, too.) However square Gould was — proudly square — he had soul and something more. Like the pop people, he knew how to wear his soul on his sleeve, how to show it. That was the first thing other musicians knew about him, and they respected him for it.

"Jazz players weren't cut off the way they are now," drummer Archie Alleyne told me. "A lot of jazz players had studied at the Conservatory. I'd say every musician in town had heard about Glenn Gould. Word was he had Oscar Peterson's technique but played classical." In fact, over the years, one CBC producer or another would imagine bringing Peterson and Gould together for a TV special. "Maybe I'll play a little classical," Peterson told me when I brought it up with him during an interview. Gould replied to a request from one producer, saying "it would be a great pleasure to meet with Mr. Peterson at any time, because, even though I'm very much out of my depth in relation to the jazz field, I have the highest regard for his remarkable ability."

In the mid-1960s, rock 'n' rollers across Canada began hearing a pounding new single called "Brainwashed" by a band called D.C. Thomas and the Bossmen on CHUM and other rock stations. D.C. Thomas, a tough kid from the Toronto suburb of Willowdale who'd done a bit of time in reformatories, would by the late sixties reinvent himself as David Clayton-Thomas to lead Blood, Sweat and Tears to huge rock success. But "Brainwashed" reflects Clayton-Thomas in his early punky prime, singing a rocker given a jolt by a pair of piano solos, seemingly dropped in from nowhere, revealing a fabulous technique and the influence of Glenn Gould's Bach. Anyone curious at the time would have discovered that the solo came from Tony Collacott, who happened to be a student of Myrtle Rose Guerrero, Alberto's second wife, herself a student of Wanda Landowska and Alfred Cortot.

In his brilliant but brief career, playing jazz for the most part — he was also part of Chimo!, another short-lived local band — Collacott was forever called "the Glenn Gould of jazz." If nothing else, Gould's technique was worth copying.

Actually, Gould was into his own sort of jazz. In his 1964 lecture to the graduating class at the RCM, he talked about practising some Mozart at his home when he was thirteen — a familiar enough activity for the young crowd at hand — when the family's cleaning lady turned on the vacuum cleaner. The louder passages in the Mozart suddenly "became surrounded with a halo of vibrato," he told the graduates. The softer parts couldn't be heard at all.

"Those parts which I couldn't actually hear sounded best of all."

Thelonious Monk could not have said it better.

FIRST HE TAKES MANHATTAN

Columbia Records' signing of Glenn Gould on January 12, 1955, was one of the great leaps of corporate faith in the music business. Here was an unknown Canadian pianist, working with a little-known

Recording sheet for *The Goldberg Variations*.

manager — a manager from Toronto, yet — without a game plan. Well, almost without a game plan. Walter Homburger, a Toronto concert impresario since 1947, had begun to make plans with the Gould family to take Manhattan years earlier, but he delayed until he felt Glenn was ready. Having blown away Canadian audiences, Glenn was now ready. Following the Broadway tradition of opening the show out of town, the Goulds rented the Phillips Gallery in Washington, D.C., on January 2, 1955, for their son's American debut.

A cocky Glenn Gould offered up a challenging repertoire that included Webern and Beethoven, and earned a career-making review from the *Washington Post*'s Paul Hume: "We know of no other pianist like him at any age."

Gould's second U.S. concert was on January 11 at New York's Town Hall, which he'd rented for $450. A small crowd of music insiders and fellow pianists showed up, a few of them informed by their Toronto friends of the phenomenon they were about to witness. This concert attracted

Standard practice: soak arm carefully.

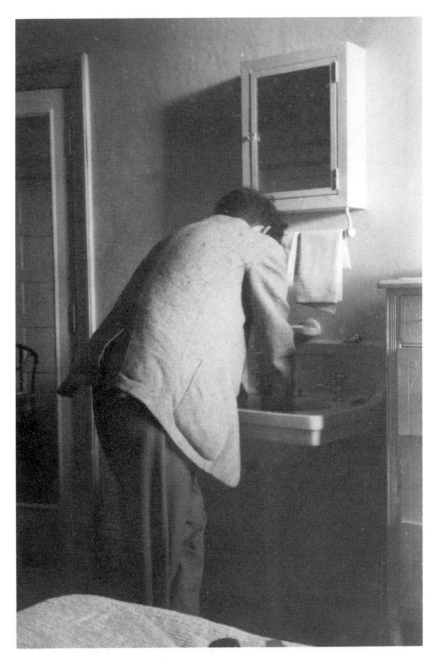

Standard practice: use lots of hot water.

New York's second-string music critics, and not many of them. One noted Gould's "powers as a technician," but that was pretty much it.

David Oppenheim, head of the artist and repertoire division for Columbia Records' Masterworks, was at Town Hall, though. The next day he offered Gould a contract, an unprecedented signing based on a single debut performance. By June 10, 1955, Gould was in Columbia's 30th Street recording studio, an acoustic gem created inside a former church building, recording *The Goldberg Variations*. Lasting through to June 16, the session left the impression that the kid knew what he was doing.

Columbia's three-year contract — the label's first signing of a Canadian — was relatively modest by all accounts: Gould himself grumbled for some time about what he didn't get. But it proved to be an absolute windfall. By 1960 Gould's *Goldberg* had sold an estimated 40,000 copies, a staggering number for a classical release at the time. Gould griped that Homburger hadn't extracted more money from Columbia, which was having one banner year after another. Nevertheless, he stayed with the company for the rest of his recording life, although he told friends in the late seventies that he wanted to leave. Columbia, for its part, gave him freedom of choice about what to record (anything he wanted, pretty much), where to record it (Toronto more often than not in the later years), and whenever it suited him. Maintaining his independence was one of Gould's greatest triumphs at the label. It was one of the company's, too. Glenn Gould's second *Goldberg* of 1981 had sold more than two million copies by the year 2000 against a background of cratering classical sales and the rise of digital downloading.

But we should back up a bit. The reasons leading to this game-changing recording — was any debut recording in classical music history more unforeseen? — have remained vague for years. Gould was never particularly helpful himself about the reasons, remaining tactically obtuse on the matter. (When facts about Glenn Gould seem fogged over, you might be right in guessing he's the fog-maker.) At one point Gould explained he simply wanted to do something "that for the most part had not been committed to disc." And, yes, *The Goldberg Variations* once did qualify somewhat in that regard, although the work was hardly unknown. Rosalyn Tureck's *Goldberg*, recorded in 1947 but released in 1949, was well known and much admired.

Gould further explained in a 1959 interview with Alan Rich that it was one of the first pieces he learned "entirely" without Alberto Guerrero's input, although that's difficult to take at face value given that his teacher performed the work and had taught it to other students. Why wouldn't Guerrero pass it by Glenn Gould, by far the greatest Bach player of all of his students? Perhaps the piece was the first work Gould adopted for his own in-depth study, entirely on his own volition and not because his teacher had led the way.

But there's another fact Gould gave Rich that I find far more interesting. It's the year Gould said he began to study the piece — 1950 — a signpost for the time frame when he grew to be particularly focused on the work. But why 1950? Here's one possible answer.

On March 21, 1950, John Beckwith, a fellow Guerrero pupil and one of Gould's closest friends at the time, although five years older, gave a performance/lecture called "Bach: *The Goldberg Variations*" at the Royal Ontario Museum Theatre, rented by Beckwith himself for the occasion. Tickets were $1.20, with a "limited number of student tickets at half price." The small, captivated, knowledgeable crowd on hand included Glenn Gould.

Beckwith's model for performance/lecture was that given years earlier by Donald Francis Tovey, the influential British musicologist and performer, whose much-admired published work was taken from notes he'd given at performances. "I'd admired Tovey," Beckwith told me. "I thought I was a sort of a smart-ass in doing what he did too, because other pianists were not doing that. Actually, I was quite green, although I was playing piano quite well at the time."

Gould would have appreciated the particular resonance that came with Beckwith's chosen date: it was Bach's birthday. (Beckwith had given much the same lecture at an earlier date in Hamilton, Ontario.) Following the event, Gould caught up to Beckwith backstage and was, in Beckwith's memory of the moment, particularly effusive in his congratulations.

"Of course, our teacher Guerrero had played the *Goldberg* in several performances in the mid-thirties," Beckwith went on to tell me in his serene downtown Toronto house, where two high-end bikes display Beckwith's extra-musical interest. "I had studied it with him, which was very helpful. So it wasn't something I picked up out of the blue. Guerrero was very much a Bach specialist. All his students had to study Bach. Had to? He didn't *make* you do anything, but it was an emphasis."

Beckwith's presence in Canadian music history is unmatched if relatively unknown beyond professional music circles (*Unheard Of* is the snarky title of Beckwith's memoir). In an era when composers doubled up on jobs as teachers or administrators or print music critics or broadcasters, he excelled in each field: as an accomplished pianist and composer of some 130 works; as an academic — he was my music history professor for a term or two; and as an administrator, serving as dean of the Faculty of Music, University of Toronto. What I remember best is how the lucidity of his thinking was evident in everything he did. (Beckwith praised Bach for being "just as subtle and explicit in his title pages as he was in his music.") The same clarity of structure and sonorities in Beckwith's *Trumpets of Summer* of 1964 — with a libretto by Margaret Atwood, who was still a doctoral student — appear as well in his music criticism, which perhaps inevitably caused him to pan the great Glenn Gould in print when Beckwith felt Gould was off-track. (The pair began sniping at each other following Beckwith's performance on the CBC of Aaron Copland's 1941 Sonata, which Gould let be known he didn't particularly like.)

"His Mozart was a travesty," Beckwith says. "Everyone said so. But he ended up saying, 'Oh, I had more fun with that than I ever had before.' Actually, Mozart was his real rival. His career was set to beat Mozart and he wanted to spend his later career composing. He would give up public piano playing — which he did — and he would write music. Well, he found that to write music wasn't that easy. Writing his String Quartet was literally bar by bar."

What's interesting (and what's weird) about any of Gould's reflections on Mozart is how bitchy they sound. Gould didn't get Bartok either, but was never bitchy about it. But if Gould ever had a kinky relationship it was with Mozart. He couldn't stay away from Mozart, performing his work frequently. But Gould couldn't much stay with Mozart either — *with him* in the sense of doing what Mozart wanted done with his music. Gould's Mozart inevitably drew unpleasant criticism, which wasn't softened following an interview the pianist gave *Newsweek* in which he proclaimed, "I'd have to say that Mozart died too late rather than too early." (Ironically and horribly, the same was said of Gould.)

Recognizing the outrage-driven ratings possibilities here, the *Public Broadcasting Laboratory* series by National Educational Television, the precursor to PBS in the United States, broadcast Gould's thirty-seven-minute-long *How Mozart Became a Bad Composer* on April 28, 1968. After that, the show disappeared from sight worldwide, and a version of the script was only uncovered years later by New York–based documentarian Lucille Carra. What she found was that in his script for the show Gould felt that Mozart later in life came to rely too much on his facility for improvisation. "Why were those prodigious gifts which made Mozart as a young man the toast of Europe, reduced, in the end, to skilful parody?" Gould writes.

But is he writing about himself?

Like many of Gould's other early friendships, this one with Beckwith ended with Gould breaking off ties, and with Beckwith not being entirely forgiving. (Beckwith got riled when he saw that Gould was being called "the last puritan" by so many admirers when he was having an affair in the late 1960s with Cornelia Foss, "another man's wife," says Beckwith.)

In speaking with me Beckwith was circumspect about leaving an impression he might have influenced Gould in any way. Then again, history had to be served. Yes, he, Beckwith, created radio collage pieces in the early sixties with the celebrated Canadian poet James Reaney, in which words acted as sound and vice versa. This was well before Gould took much the same route. And yes, Beckwith's entrepreneurial abilities at promoting and funding his own performances might have given Gould thoughts along the same line in 1952, when he and Robert Fulford formed New Music Associates. On October 16, 1954, the third and final Associates concert featured Maureen Forrester in her local debut and Gould's first public performance of *The Goldberg Variations*, which likely reached as far south as New York and Columbia Records when ballyhooed through the musical grapevine.

Gould and Fulford's relationship as young intellectuals about town went far beyond music and into, among other things, politics. "One of the most exciting periods we had together was during the American political election of 1948, when [Democrat Harry S.] Truman won and [Republican Thomas E.] Dewey didn't. It was all over the radio — we didn't have television at the time — and he'd come out with his lists, and I had mine, about who's going to win California, that kind of thing. For only people like Truman could possibly be allowed to win — Glenn and me being obviously liberal Canadian kids."

Gould was fascinated with print media, Fulford's milieu. For his part, Fulford, an omnivorous reader, found his way through Gould's world, discovering writing about Schoenberg, Berg, and Webern. When Gould broached the idea of the modernist concert series — he as the musical director, his friend Robert as everything else — they both knew they were heading into relatively uncharted territory. "He knew there'd be a couple of hundred people who'd come to the concerts," Fulford tells me in his airy study overlooking the ravine running through Toronto's tony Rosedale district, the roof of the Studio Building where the Group of Seven painted partially visible through the trees.

"But he still had a lot of confidence in himself, and he wasn't yet known around the world. So when it came to planning for *The Goldberg Variations*, everybody was excited about it. It was going to be a big thing, even if for only two hundred people. It was really important."

Gould's *Goldberg Variations* remains on a different level of discussion from the radio works and musical promotion. "You can't turn it off," said Beckwith. Nevertheless, some further evidence of Gould's debt to Beckwith for framing the special place held by Bach's *Variations* in music history comes when you compare Beckwith's typewritten lecture on the work with Gould's liner notes for the original Columbia LP (ML 5060) release.

The quasi-religious aura hovering still around Bach obscures his inherent entrepreneurialism, which extended to his practice as a composer. Put simply, Bach's keyboard works were display pieces for his own virtuosity. He "at length acquired such a high degree of facility — '*hoher Grad von Fertigkeit*' — and, we may almost say, unlimited power over his instrument in all the keys that difficulties almost ceased to exist for him," wrote Johann Nikolaus Forkel in *Über Johann Sebastian Bachs Leben, Kunst und Kunstwerke* (*J.S. Bach's Life, Art and Work*). Published

Master tape of Columbia Masterworks LP ML 5060: *The Goldberg Variations.*

in Leipzig in 1802, it was Bach's first biography. *The Goldberg Variations* was his biggest keyboard hit as well as the only keyboard work published in his lifetime (in 1741).

But Both Beckwith and Gould place near the beginning of their notes a story from Forkel. The narrative concerns the wealthy Count Hermann Karl von Keyserling (spellings differ) who, unable to sleep, asked Bach for some music that Johann Gottlieb Goldberg, one of the count's court musicians, might play to soothe the princely nerves after the frazzled count had retired for the night. Bach turned to an unassuming saraband he'd sketched out some fifteen years earlier for the *Anna Magdalena Notebooks* — an uncomplicated melody stretched over a frequently used form of a bass line — to function as the aria and the thematic kernel for the subsequent thirty different variations.

The depth and range of emotion in *The Goldberg Variations* drawn out by Bach from his little musical gift to his second wife is extraordinary and near-unprecedented. Probably the only similarly prodigious elaboration on something so modest is *À la recherche du temps perdu* (*Remembrance of Things Past*), in which the memory of Marcel Proust's narrator is flooded with a life's worth of sensations after he bites into a sugary *petite madeleine* cake. American pianist Jeremy Denk understood the Proustian nature of the *Goldbergs* when he wrote: "*The Goldbergs*, insular and obsessed, have all the failings of classical music in general. The piece is a text reflecting on itself, satisfied in its own world, suggesting that everything you would ever want to know is contained within. The variations (by definition music about music) are subject to countless insider discussions in the outer world."

Beckwith wonders simply, "How can this be the theme for a set of 30 variations?" Gould wonders, too, about the same thing — "the baffling incongruity between the imposing dimensions of the variations and the unassuming variation which conceived them."

Later, Gould, like Beckwith before him, mentions Ralph Kirkpatrick, the great American harpsichordist and scholar whose 1938 edition of the *Goldbergs* for music publisher G. Schirmer in New York remains definitive. Like Beckwith, Gould uses for illustration one of Kirkpatrick's architectural allusions. Gould, like Beckwith again, turns to literature to summarize. Beckwith suggests how Bach's *Goldberg* aria "contains the spirit of all the variations, just as the meaning of the first line of a great poem is enhanced by the suggestions of the later lines." Gould in his later Columbia recording notes that this is "music which observes neither end nor beginning, with neither real climax nor real resolution, music which, like Baudelaire's lovers, 'rests lightly on the wings of the unchecked wind.'"

For Columbia Records, though, Gould's *Goldberg* sessions provided the template for the publicity department to define Gould for all and for ever. Here was the kooky guy from Up North everyone had heard rumours about, all bundled up on "a balmy June day." He brought with him five

Going into the famed Columbia Records 30th Street Studio.

pill bottles ("all different colours and descriptions"), soaked his hands in scalding hot water prior to playing, and hummed along as he played. This was the stuff of a press department's dreams. The publicists were unaware of what Gould really was up to, that he was putting his stamp on the very recording process itself, a hard-to-sell idea at the best of times.

The universal industry practice of recording with tape — lacquered discs were abandoned industry-wide around 1950 — was ready-made for Glenn Gould, the emerging young genius of studio manipulation and what he called "take-two-ness" (or take-three-ness, or ...). Yet, in recording his *Goldberg Variations* in the breakneck time of thirty-eight minutes and thirty-four seconds — the piece sounding even more succinct because of his decision not to play the repeats — Gould, the consummate parodist, flouted the new LP technology's promise of greater recording length by condensing his own recording time. (Angela Hewitt's 1999 *Goldberg* is some forty minutes longer. Gould's own second *Goldberg* in 1981 is fifty-one minutes and eighteen seconds).

The slow opening aria was the final section to be laid down in the week of recording. It required twenty-one takes before Gould was satisfied. The difficulty was not in providing what was needed, but in absenting what was not wanted. Gould said he wanted the aria to have a "sufficiently neutral" character and "not to prejudge the depth of involvement that comes later in the work."

Neutral is a loaded word. Neutral is anything but neutral, signalling the dynamic undoing of opposing ideas, structures, and beliefs, as Roland Barthes explored in one his famous series of lectures at the Collège de France from 1977 to 1978. In Barthes's telling, neutral is a sort of no man's land between opposing elements. In editing his *Goldberg* from back to front, as it were, Gould aimed to expunge from the aria anything that might allow the listener to decode the rest of the work, neutralizing expectations or comparison. In a way he's erasing the idea of "interpretation" from the work. "It is, in short, music which observes neither end nor beginning, music with neither real climax nor real resolution," he claimed in his back-cover essay on *The Goldberg Variations*. (A number of the outtakes from the first *Goldberg* are included in an edition of the two *Goldbergs* released as a box set called *A State of Wonder*, which includes a staged, Gould-directed interview the pianist had with critic Tim Page. Both *Goldbergs*, 1955 and 1981, have been reissued on audiophile 180 gram vinyl. The 1981 version was transferred from a newly discovered analogue master tape.)

In writing the 1964 radio piece he adapted for his his article "The Prospects of Recording," Gould quotes Marshall McLuhan. "The meaning of experience is typically one generation behind the experience — the content of new situations, both private and corporate, is typically the preceding situation — the first stage of mechanical culture became aware of agrarian values and pursuits — the first age of the planter glorified the hunt — and the first stage of electronic culture (the day of the telegraph and the telephone) glorified the machine as an art form." In a sense, the forward-looking Gould was also looking back to the triumphant if narrow-focused reception given to his *Goldberg*. While "enormous" technique attracted universal raves, the press wasn't entirely sure what exactly he had accomplished, though they predicted a stellar future. "The music appears to mean something to him," said the *Times*'s Harold C. Schonberg. "Further revelations are to be expected," announced *Newsweek*. Gould's *Goldberg* not only made it inevitable he was a concert dropout: it made it a certainty.

An aside: the full influence of McLuhan's thinking on Gould, while evident in a tangential way in a lot of his writing, was never addressed by Gould himself. And this never made complete sense to me, in that they were neighbours for a bit, liked and admired each other, and were downtown Toronto men whose paths crossed repeatedly. One of the most iconic photos in Canadian history was taken in 1967 by the *Toronto Telegram* and shows novelist Morley Callaghan, conductor Sir Ernest MacMillan, actress Kate Reid, and Group of Seven artist A.Y. Jackson walking across a windswept plain with Gould and McLuhan just to their left. *Kate Reid: On the Bluffs* is the title of the shot. But it's the sight of McLuhan and Gould, somewhat off on their own, having left the others in their wake, that suggests something unique about their relationship. Then there are the stories of Gould showing up at the McLuhan residence to thump out something on the family piano. But most McLuhan family members insist that this never happened, according to Philip

Marchand, whose 1998 biography, *Marshall McLuhan: The Medium and the Messenger*, brings considerable clarity to the chaotic world surrounding McLuhan. For a while I was a part of that world and the special McLuhan-hosted evening courses at the University of Toronto. In fact, I submitted a paper, its fate still unknown. The Great Man appeared only occasionally and never enough to rein in the McLuhanese babble going on all around.

To Marchand, Gould and McLuhan were media rivals. "I do feel on sure ground comparing McLuhan and Gould as performers who gravitated to the centre of attention," Philip told me over lunch. Marchand was an affable *Toronto Star* colleague for many years; we retired the same day. "In Gould's case," Marchand continued, "it was via the piano. In McLuhan's case it was via verbal performances. McLuhan's mother was a professional entertainer, it must not be forgotten, an elocutionist in an era prior to radio and television, and McLuhan honed his intellectual skills on verbal jousts over the kitchen table."

One other thing: McLuhan wasn't particularly musical. Saying he had a tin ear would be unkind, but not that far off the mark, I've been told.

THE KING

Masterworks had a distinguished roster of musicians well before signing Gould, including Walter Gieseking, the great French-born Mozart and Debussy specialist, then experiencing a comeback years after his stay in Nazi Germany during the Second World War. Goddard Lieberson, head of classical music at Columbia during its glory years from the 1950s to the early 1970s, was adding artists who might attract interest beyond the classical market, including Leonard Bernstein, who was well on his way to becoming a household name, and Oscar Levant, a concert pianist-turned-comic who starred with Gene Kelly in *An American in Paris*, Vincente Minnelli's 1951 musical. Columbia had also cornered the market on the Broadway musical soundtrack with *Kiss Me Kate* (1948) and *South Pacific* (1949), and with both the 1957 stage version of *West Side Story* and the 1961 film version of the Bernstein musical.

The sexy look of genius.

Lieberson's patrician manner masked a populist thinker with a perceptive sense of American popular culture. He'd been a nightclub pianist at one time and wrote for a newspaper. With TV now in almost every home, Lieberson knew that marketing music, music of every kind, had changed. New Rule No. 1: get your act on one of the live shows. Rule No. 2: get press coverage. In both instances Columbia was being outflanked by a canny ex-trucker named Elvis Presley, whose life and career were about to remake all of pop culture with his November 22, 1955, signing to RCA Victor Records, Columbia's hated archrival.

As far as we know, Presley's and Gould's paths never crossed. A media-mediated symbiotic relationship existed between the two of them, however, which extended beyond their dependencies on pills, mothers, and domineering personal managers, their night-crawling work habits, and their inner circles of hard-core, loyal friends. Like Gould, Presley had that hermit's need for sanctuary in the studio, where his genius, every bit the equal of the pianist's, harnessed the full potential of playbacks and editing to sharpen and refine even the most thrown-off sounding "uh-huh." Presley, three years younger than Gould, also found reason enough to abandon live performance in the early sixties at the peak of his career, in his case to make movies in Hollywood.

The degree their sexuality was groomed for media consumption was another shared attribute. Presley's media sex play was par for the course for a pop star: think Rudy Vallee, Duke Ellington, or Frank Sinatra. But Gould's wasn't, or at least it wasn't noticed in the greater Gouldian universe, where it was tactfully ignored by his handlers and press alike in favour of the unfolding of the deeper, more serious narrative as was expected with a classical music star.

Larger-than-life, young and sexy classical piano players have a long and star-studded history: Henri Herz, Franz Liszt, Ignacy Jan Paderewski. Their impact depended on live performances, their sexual reputation an accumulation of their conquests after gigs. But Gould's sexuality was new to classical music — at least at the time — in how it played out in the mass media, time and time again. On stage he might be the shabby slacker in rumpled clothes (Liszt was considered "very negligent in his attire" early on in his career, or so conductor Charles Hallé observed). Or Gould might stuff himself into an ill-fitting tuxedo, a gesture of camaraderie with the tux-wearing orchestra members. But beyond the concert stage, he was the definition of cool, an adult playing out a teen dream of stardom with a rock 'n' roller's moves scaled for a classical music concert.

Presley's sullen, sneakily aggressive, lip-curled sexuality was his calling card and was immediately understood — the nice boy ("Yes'm") with the simmering hots for the nice girl next door. Gould's sexuality felt more subversive because it was deemed to be off-limits, even when discussed by other musicians, a notoriously lubricious lot. Gould's overt interest in women was hardly a secret, at least to the women involved. Several female musicians and music school friends of mine reported having long midnight conversations with him and thought nothing of it. Or they said they thought nothing of it. "We just talked, that's all," one told me. "That's all that came of it."

Enough whispering went on to squelch rumours gaining traction at the time that he was gay or — much worse — asexual. (Years back, when I was told I was on the shortlist for a Gould biography, I asked if there were any no-go zones when it came to his life, "like, you know, he was gay." Nothing was said. The inner circle vetting me gave me that smile that said, "You poor fool.")

Even his media-readiness was, in its own way, subversive. He gave more than he was asked for: he shaped the photo shoot. He knew how "they" — photographers, marketers, newspaper editors — liked to show him, and he learned to model for just the image wanted: a mop of hair fallen over his eyes, leaning back on his piano stool and languidly elongating his slender body, draping his hands just so, revealing the long, long fingers, muscular yet beautiful. Let the critics rattle on about the truth beyond his "sharp, clear technique," a description by Harold C. Schonberg in the *New York Times*. To *Vogue*, he looked "emaciated," a major bonus for a fashion magazine, "with blueberry blue eyes." Such media-friendliness has been standard operating procedure ever since, from punk-styled classical fiddler Nigel Kennedy to pianist Yuja Wang with her very short orange dress. Gould's success at it has kept him in the mix. A variety of contemporary websites *still* continue to give high ratings to his "hottie" potential.

MITCH

Gould had other reasons for signing with Columbia: the company's advances in audio technologies. Its recordings simply sounded more modern than other labels'. Classical music head Goddard Lieberson was one person who led the company in that direction. Mitch Miller was another.

Miller, a professional oboist by training and classmate of Lieberson at the Eastman School of Music, was hired by Lieberson in 1950 to head the artist and repertoire division of Columbia's pop department. Miller eventually became a genial American TV personality, but that was just

Selecting pianos at Columbia's 30th Street Studio.

Finding the right piano.

about appearances. He and Lieberson had revolutionized the business of making records. Lieberson, by harnessing everything Columbia recorded to the rapidly developing LP process, gave his company a considerable edge over rivals RCA and Decca. Miller knew how to maximize the unprecedentedly luxurious sound the LP was capable of. Their Columbia recording studio was an eye-opener for Glenn Gould, and as much as anything he found later at the CBC. (Gould was a tech junkie going back to his childhood hooking up a backyard tin-can phone system with his friend Robert Fulford. Gould later purchased a car phone as soon as they came on the market. No wonder he owned so much Bell stock.)

Rough, rugged, and proletarian, rock 'n' roll was emerging as the authentic alternative to the emotionless mainstream. Columbia answered rock's rawness with the electrifying modernity of emerging technology. "The Yellow Rose of Texas," a huge hit for Miller and his orchestra in 1955, sounded hopelessly square to anyone beginning to listen to rock 'n' roll. But in terms of sound, it was pure space age. The glistening surface that Miller's studio savvy lacquered onto each old-time note — the tune itself goes back at least to 1850s America — was the audio equivalent of preparing food in aspic. Hence the soaring echoes-from-space sound of Johnny Mathis's 1956 hit "Chances Are."

Columbia wasn't just in the business of producing a record. With each and every recording, it was also in the business of *selling* it to the listener. There was Barbra Streisand taking over, reframing and re-understanding "Soon It's Gonna Rain" from *The Fantasticks* and making it a hit. The pitch-purity of her singing was wrapped in more surface glitter. You got hooked on it. You joined the Columbia Record Club, as I did, to get the latest sound buzz as much as to hear the latest tracks. It benefited Glenn Gould, too, adding to the buzzy, speedy, hyper-produced feel of his records, each of the inner contrapuntal lines of his Bach as clear as crystal beneath his fingers.

Perhaps it was inevitable that Gould would work for so many years on so many recordings so successfully with Andrew Kazdin as his producer. Kazdin's relationship with Gould eventually soured and ended ignobly with Kazdin's firing. But before then Kazdin had dazzled Gould with his know-how. An MIT engineering dropout as well as a trained musician, Kazdin revolutionized symphonic recordings using multiple mikes for clarity, a pop technique. Gould marvelled at Kazdin's ability and the way he would edit in one note to replace what he felt was a lesser one. Kazdin was the face, and the ears, of modern classical recording. It was the sound of the new high fidelity.

Anyone tracking Gould's recordings from the late fifties until he stopped performing live in 1964 finds the going bumpy, a wheels-falling-off moment coming early on in his recording *Beethoven Piano Sonatas Nos. 30–32*, to be followed by album after album of wonderful Bach, as impressive as the *Goldberg* in many ways, then his Berg,

Columbia recording engineer Fred Plaut preparing mikes for Gould's 1959 recording session at Columbia's 30th Street Studio.

Schoenberg, and Krenek piano works, and then the expected beauties found in his *Brahms: 10 Intermezzi,* his eleventh recording in 1961 for Masterworks. What strikes you, though, is how modern everything is — how intelligence shines through the emerging new technologies of sound reproduction: high fidelity, FM radio, and 33 ⅓ long-playing recordings.

Hi-fi didn't happen in a vacuum. It resulted in part as fallout from corporate wars and very real shooting wars. Radio's boom in the thirties spurred corporate interest for even newer media to attract audiences on grander scales than dreamed of before. David Sarnoff, RCA's wonder boy, decided to bet the future on television and in 1935 spent $1 million on the project — a crazy amount of wasted loot, or so it was thought at the time. Believing TV would render radio irrelevant, Sarnoff relegated the latest radio development, FM, to the back burner, even though the sound quality it delivered was proven to be superior to the AM band. FM was a cult, a fusty hobby for sound-technology buffs and classical music fans. By the mid-1940s, only some forty FM stations were broadcasting in the United States. Several years later there was CKOI-FM in Montreal, Canada's first FM station.

The full, rich FM sound might have remained marginalized if not for two other tech developments: hi-fi and Columbia Records' introduction in 1948 of the long-playing record, which used vinyl. (Shellac, the main ingredient in the 78 rpm disc, was in short supply during the Second World War, leaving as an alternative something called "Vinylite," the brand name for an acid-resistant thermoplastic. Vinyl, capable of a finer groove than its older 78 rpm counterpart, allowed for up to five times the recording time on a single surface, in some cases up to twenty-eight minutes per side.)

One of war's legacies is technological advancement — radar leading to the microwave oven, that kind of thing. Another Second World War by-product was attitude, a gung-ho, do-it-yourself mindset. And so Maurice G. Kains's *Five Acres and Independence* ("the practical guide to the selection and management of a small farm"), published in 1935 and reprinted in a 1948 Pocket Books edition, convinced my parents to move to 2.5 acres of former farmland in the suburbs and grow their own vegetables, and led my dad, the piano teacher with pale hands, to build his dream house with his own hammer and bad language. The craze for do-it-yourself hi-fi units soon had newspapers and magazines featuring the latest technique or gizmo. Listening to hi-fi at home was like "gourmet cooking" — it signalled your attainment of "with-it" thinking and money (so did reading *Playboy*, founded in 1953, but that was another manner of being "with it"). Columbia Masterworks was there waiting, FM radio was ready for revival, and there was a new generation of artists who knew their way through the new audiophile world. You could say Glenn Gould was ready for *High Fidelity* magazine, launched in 1951, as it was ideal for some of his most important thinking on technology, starting with "Prospects of Recording" in April 1966.

"In an unguarded moment some months ago," he wrote, "I predicted that the public concert as we know it today would no longer exist a century hence, that its functions would have been entirely taken over by electronic media. It had not occurred to me that this statement represented a particularly radical pronouncement. Indeed, I regarded it almost as self-evident truth and, in any case, as defining only one of the peripheral effects occasioned by developments in the electronic age. But never has a statement of mine been so widely quoted — or so hotly disputed."

SZELL OUT

When not in the studio, Glenn Gould, pushed by manager Walter Homburger, was almost constantly on tour during the late 1950s and early sixties, a period that could be the basis for a great movie. Most likely, it would be *the* Glenn Gould movie: a major star enduring mysterious illnesses, epiphanies, rapturous receptions, and promises of sexual passion in the Soviet Union at the peak of the Cold War, in Europe, and in the young state of Israel. The backdrops are unique and memorable: desert wastes with Gould meditating on a sand dune — okay, in a Hertz rental car near a sand dune; German gothic architecture passed by on a train voyage to Hamburg — ill, feeling alone and suddenly alive; or Leonard Bernstein's apartment in New York, with the best and brightest of contemporary music, sharing cocktails. The film's tone is bittersweet with some borderline absurd moments. The voiceover is already written by

Adjusting the famous chair.

Gould, who kept up a steady correspondence back home. Better, there's even a darkly comic beginning with alternative versions of the story.

It was March of 1957. Gould was to make his Cleveland debut with the curmudgeonly George Szell leading the Cleveland Orchestra in Beethoven's Piano Concerto No. 2 — by now a Gould specialty, and yet another work rescued from semi-obscurity — along with the Schoenberg Piano Concerto, requested by Szell, but which he later cancelled. Gould, knowing Szell's distaste for the piece, assumed the conductor simply hadn't learned it sufficiently, so he arrived at the concert hall prepared to do only the Beethoven. This is where the story splits into competing ones: Gould's, and that of legend. There's also a mystery involved. Why did Szell want the Schoenberg if, as Gould says, he didn't show much empathy with the composer?

The legend: Gould asked an orchestra carpenter to fix little blocks beneath the piano Gould was to play to raise it ever so slightly — father Bert Gould's famous homemade chair could not be lowered — and this distracted Szell. The conductor snapped at his soloist: "Perhaps if I were to slice one-sixteenth of an inch off your derrière, Mr. Gould,

Adjusting the chair, with a little help from a friend.

Chair and occupant in full operational mode.

we could begin." Or so the yarn was reported in a *Time* cover story on Szell sometime later, and was repeated in Szell obituaries in *Time* and in slightly altered version elsewhere. Szell — whom Gould admired over Bernstein and most other conductors — also said of the pianist: "That nut's a genius," or so it was reported to Gould by Louis Lane, the Cleveland Orchestra's second conductor.

The Gould version: Yes, the carpenter was brought in, and yes, he did distract the maestro during a rehearsal break. According to Gould — as told to Jonathan Cott in *Conversations with Glenn Gould* — Szell merely asked, "Vat are you doing?" and that was that. Later there was a brief clash of wills as the Beethoven rehearsal continued, this time the second movement. Gould insisted on continuing to use a lot of soft pedal — the one used to muffle the sound significantly — while Szell felt the result was *too* soft. Lane, when asked, immediately confirmed Szell's judgment. But Gould wouldn't budge, insisting that the soft pedal made the modern piano sound more like the one Beethoven himself used. Nevertheless, Gould agreed to play a little louder while still using the soft pedal. Much later, the pianist said that if Szell had said what *Time* reported him having said, Gould would have told the orchestra to look for another soloist.

In fact, 1957 started terrifically enough with Gould's New York orchestra debut with Bernstein and the Philharmonic performing to great success the Beethoven Second Piano Concerto, later recorded by them at the 30th Street Studio, which was later coupled with their version of Bach's Keyboard Concerto No. 1.

Gould's return to Bach with the late-1957 release of his fourth album — featuring Partitas No. 5 and No. 6 and *The Well-Tempered Clavier II:* Fugues No. 9 and No. 14 — remedied whatever damage had been done to his reputation by the earlier Beethoven Sonatas release with its wild fluctuations of tempo. Yet his grinding tour schedule, while adding to a reputation for on-stage brilliance, had by then also solidified his reputation as the King of Cancellations. Gould's reputation was salvaged somewhat back in Toronto by manager Homburger's ability to feed the media — particularly the *Toronto Star* — with news of each of his client's fresh triumphs.

~

There *is*, in fact, a Gould-on-tour movie, Yosif Feyginberg's *Glenn Gould: The Russian Journey.* One might wonder what to expect given the year of the Gould trip (1957) and the date of the fifty-seven-minute film's release (2002). But one's expectations are exceeded.

Gould arrived in Moscow on May 5 with Homburger — who was "on assignment" as a special correspondent for the *Toronto Star* — and several dozen copies of the *Goldberg* to be given away as gifts. *Russian Journey* showcases the radiant sense of self and entitlement Gould exuded at the time, which sparked excitement wherever he went. The soundtrack consists of rare made-in-Moscow recordings as well as a never-before-released recording of his Leningrad lecture/recital. Insider stuff on the politics involved — Moscow trying to woo Ottawa away from the United States during the deepest freeze in the Cold War — came from obscure documents in the Canadian Ministry of Foreign Affairs (Van Cliburn arrived in Moscow the year after Gould). But the heart of the film is Gould, only twenty-four years old and at the very peak of his public career — not only as a performer, but as a public figure still hungry for a public. And Gould being Gould, he demanded a place to sleep at the Canadian embassy because he disliked the bed in the hotel he was given.

News of the *Goldberg*'s tumultuous reception had yet to reach the Soviet Union. So there was only a modest turnout at the beginning of his all-Bach May 7 debut Soviet concert in the Great Hall of the Moscow Conservatory. Modest, that is, before the break. At half-time, the flurry of "you-can't-miss-this" phone calls resulted in an overflow crowd for the second half. Soviet musicians had in previous generations thought of Bach as some sort of dour choirmaster. In Gould's hands, he was another composer entirely. In the days that followed, Gould attained rock star status: he later said he felt as if he'd landed on Mars or Venus. A who's who of Soviet music stars turned out to meet him. Added seats were needed for his May 14 and 16 Leningrad appearances.

His lecture/recitals, centred on Schoenberg and Viennese atonality — forbidden territory under Soviet cultural dictates — were talked about for years. For all his success in Europe or across North America, Gould had never seen anything like it. He even found a moment of benediction when Heinrich Neuhaus, the aging but still-dominant teacher of emerging Soviet piano stars — Emil Gilels and the hammering Sviatoslav Richter among them — said, more or less, that Glenn Gould was the best. More than a mere pianist, Neihaus wrote, Gould "is a phenomenon."

Years later Gould told a film crew, "I hope to go back to Russia." But by then his distaste for touring — or being a tourist, which he was "bad at" — had, for the most part, checkmated any further on-the-road adventures.

LENNIE

Of all the controversies in Gould's controversy-ridden career, his 1962 performances of Brahms's Piano Concerto No. 1 in D minor, Op. 15, with Leonard Bernstein and the New York Philharmonic on April 5, 6, and 8 top just about any list. One might rightly now ask why. At the time, though, the answer was thought to be evident. Here was Glenn Gould, pre-eminent eccentric in all of classical music, pulling the plug on the usually electrifying Brahms First so that it seemed to flow in slo-mo. The first movement felt like the second; the enormous emotional peaks and valleys had become a single straightaway. And it was seemingly done with Bernstein's complicity. The result: a dry, studious interpretation forced upon a great if reluctant orchestra, a band led previously to undreamed of heights by Mahler and Toscanini, an institution for which families kept their season tickets for generations. Gould's well-known, well-honed dislike of New York City contributed to the atmosphere, too. Playing New York was a breeze, he'd let it be known. Playing in Toronto — now that gave a bad case of nerves.

The story does, in fact, begin in Canada. The first Gould–Brahms First connection began years earlier, in 1959, with Gould's debut public performance of the work in Winnipeg with Canadian conductor Victor Feldbrill leading the Winnipeg Symphony Orchestra. Feldbrill, an indefatigable presence in Canadian music since the 1940s, had met Gould a few years earlier when Feldbrill was first violinist for the Toronto Symphony. ("He was eight years younger than me, but twenty years older in other ways," Feldbrill told me a while back. The maestro was ninety-two at the time we talked, his memory sharp. He still would have liked to get up on the podium.)

Feldbrill could use Gould's star power for ticket sales. He also wanted to make a musical mark with his orchestra, particularly as he was the first Canadian conductor in its brief history. And the Winnipeg performance represented the hundredth anniversary of the First's premiere in Hanover with Brahms as soloist. Feldbrill remembered Gould playing Strauss's Burleske for Piano and Orchestra in D minor, Strauss's only piano concerto, and its mood of "European nostalgia," as Feldbrill described it. The Brahms spoke to him in much the same way, besides having in common with the Strauss the key of D minor. Orchestral writing was new territory for Brahms when he was composing the piece. And his emotions were in turmoil. A number of Brahms biographers have speculated that the 1854 suicide attempt by the horribly depressed Robert Schumann, a close, older friend, extended into Brahms's thinking. The concerto's almost gnarly, awkward opening chords slowly loosen up an unravelling of feelings. The work, which came in fits and starts to the young composer still trying to find his way with the concerto form, was finished in 1858, two years after Schumann's death.

"But it's not in Glenn's repertoire," Walter Homburger, Gould's manager, told Feldbrill.

"Still, it's what I want," said Feldbrill, typically stubborn.

"Well, all I can do is phone and ask him," said the Toronto impresario.

Homburger wasn't hopeful, not with his number one client for years now telling everyone who'd listen of his plans to quit the concert stage, and not learning new repertoire for it. To Homburger's surprise, Gould said he'd do it.

"I don't know whether Glenn wanted to rethink the piece or not," Feldbrill says. "But the performance itself" — on October 8, 1959 — "was quite spectacular, aside from a blooper from a French horn near the end," Feldbrill remembered. (Recorded live, it's still available on the Winnipeg Symphony Orchestra website.) "Brahms can sound a bit mushy. It's not Brahms's fault. It's the interpreters' fault, with ritardandos on top of ritardandos [passages marked increasingly slower]. But Glenn's performance was beautifully expressive without being mushy. He showed he had a great understanding of the architecture of the work. In looking back, the version he recorded with me wasn't that much faster than the version he did with Bernstein. I do know that Glenn did some strange things as he got older. And I do feel the Bernstein version was ponderous. It didn't move. Yet one thing remained: when Glenn played there was that great clarity."

Gould's career and Feldbrill's rarely crossed, despite the fact that they were contemporaries. Feldbrill studied conducting with French-born great Pierre Monteux in the summers of 1949 and 1950, and composition with atonalistic composer John Weinzweig. Feldbrill was another complete musician, a fine fiddler and solid administrator. But Glenn Gould was a genius. The orbit of his performing career was international and brought him closer to Leonard Bernstein. Bernstein had the panache, the intellect, the humanity, and the inquisitive musicality that Gould admired.

So Glenn and Lennie hung out. When Bernstein was in Toronto, Gould gave him a late-evening tour of the city. Bernstein later remembered being bombarded during the drive by Petula Clark music and smothering blasts from the car heater. Gould on occasion ended up in Bernstein's New York apartment when he was on his own and looking as if he needed a bit of family life — Bernstein's wife, Felicia, in her maternal mode, helped Gould wash his scruffy, well-pawed hair on one occasion. During a later Bernstein cocktail party the non-drinker Gould had a drink, only to feel absolutely wretched the next day.

Bernstein was in a select circle of performers, Yehudi Menuhin being another, whom Gould considered comrades-in-concert. Bernstein's gay friends liked to assume there might be something more to it, but there's nothing in Bernstein's extensive diary-keeping — at least what's been published to date — to suggest any liaison with Gould. One former Columbia Records executive told me if there was any passion, it was all "in Bernstein's mind." (Bernstein might kiss someone, straight or gay, enthusiastically without thinking about the consequences, the executive recalls.)

Of course the potential for superb record sales, a public relations bonanza, and dynamically artistic recordings was reason enough for Columbia Records to have its two pre-eminent classical stars paired professionally, either live or on record. Both had personas larger than the music itself, and both were capable of shifting roles at will, from leader to follower. They even had their own repartee down. Earlier, in 1960, when Gould was about to perform Beethoven's Second Piano Concerto, Bernstein asked about the tempo of the first movement.

"I feel it conducts in a fast four," Gould said. (The reporter watching all this was Joseph Roddy of the *New Yorker*.)

"I've never conducted it in four before, because I've never conducted it before," Bernstein said. "This is a Bernstein premiere."

"I have an idea — thought of it last night," Gould said. "Let's walk out there together, and you play the piano part and I'll conduct the orchestra. It will be the surprise act of the season."

So when Gould phoned Bernstein weeks before they were to perform the to-be-infamous Brahms First, Bernstein was well prepared for Gould to come up with a new approach, however radical, that the two might undertake together for the concerts.

Slow, Glenn warned Bernstein. His approach was going to be very deliberate: reining in the tempos of the traditionally dynamic first movement to the point where it was paced at the speed of the second movement. Bernstein guessed this was likely another example of Gould following some inner compositional structure that had eluded every other Brahms First player before him. Indeed, Gould was rethinking how to approach late Romanticism in general and in particular the cheap thrills it made so attractive. He gave a seductively lingering performance of Wagner's *Siegfried Idyll*, in perhaps the only way he could, by bringing out the underlying structure of the music, the skeleton, and not the great sonic heart-swelling clashes. Among a few late-nineteenth-century composers, it was Brahms — whose delicious Intermezzi were already being counted among Gould's greatest recordings — who offered sufficient structural complexity to warrant Gould's closest attention.

Brahms was the avatar of the classical side of the great Romantic movement and as such was beloved by the anti-Wagnerians, such as the formidable Viennese critic Eduard Hanslick. Brahms's particular indebtedness to Bach — bits like the reference to Bach's Cantata BMV 150 in the last movement of his Fourth Symphony — has been attracting recent academic interest. So Brahms's First Concerto is particularly inviting to a soloist with an analytical mind like Gould's, because it starts with a puzzle — a great twisted chord built above its basis on a low C-sharp note teetering over D, the work's home key, that demands a decoding to move on. But where? And over what period of time? There's no imagining Gould reacting to so much hidden information other than by decoding it.

Introspective performances by Hélène Grimaud often have the French-born pianist compared to Gould (she, too, is passionate about animals, particularly wolves and their conservation). To her, she once explained, the Brahms First is "'a requiem' to Robert Schumann's suicidal brush with death." It's "like a symphony with a piano obbligato. I've always liked having the feeling of being part of the orchestral mass."

Gould's preparation to perform the Brahms in Winnipeg was only the beginning of his exploration, which, typically, might not stop at any one discovery. Those ready to defend the Gould-Bernstein travesty point out that it was an experiment of sorts, by Gould if not Bernstein, and that Gould played the Brahms in a much more conventional manner shortly afterward in Baltimore. Nevertheless, the impending New York Phil performance was preceded by a buzz of anticipation. Gould always seemed unsettled to most non-Canadian audiences, orchestras, and critics. Increasingly, he was unsettling as well as unsettled.

"Now, don't give up," Bernstein told his players away from Gould. "Because this is a great man whom we have to take very seriously."

The orchestra, exhausted after rehearsal, didn't give up. Nor did Bernstein quit questioning Gould about the tempo, according to his memoirs.

"Are you sure you're still convinced about the 'slowth' of the piece?"

"Oh, more than ever," Gould said. "Did you hear how wonderfully the tension built?"

By tradition, the Philharmonic's Thursday concerts were less formal than those later in the week, with Bernstein offering verbal program notes on the music and the interpretation to follow — "a kind of dress rehearsal," the conductor explained later. Bernstein, having already quieted a potentially unhappy orchestra, needed to remind their audience that whatever else it felt it was witnessing a genius at work.

"So I said to Glenn backstage, 'You know, I have to talk to the people. How would it be if I warned them it was going to be very slow, and prepare them for it? Because if they didn't know they really might leave. I'll just tell them that there is a disagreement about the tempi between us, but that because of the sportsmanship element in music I would like to go along with your tempo and try it,'" Bernstein wrote later.

"It wasn't meant to be a disclaimer," Bernstein wrote. "I was very much interested in the results — particularly the audience reaction to it. I wrote down a couple of notes on the back of an envelope and showed them to Glenn. 'Is that okay?'"

"Oh, it's wonderful," Bernstein remembered Gould saying. "What a great idea."

New York critics leading the way, some think that what happened this night was an absolute fiasco partially smoothed over by both participants. But who was playing whom — beyond some Brahms, that is?

"This small disclaimer," is how Bernstein prefaced his remarks to his audience, leaving one to wonder what Bernstein's game was all about. Was the conductor covering his own reputation, being a bit two-faced in all of this? Gould would later tell a friend that he found Bernstein's speech "completely charming."

Gould's Brahms should be heard, Bernstein went on further to tell his audience, because Gould was "so valid and serious as an artist."

"What am I doing conducting it?" Bernstein asked, before suggesting that only once before was he forced to bow "to a soloist's wholly new and incompatible concept, and that was the last time I accompanied Mr. Gould."

The fallout from this has continued over the years. Comparisons of Gould's version of Brahms's First with those of other pianists show that Gould's pacing was not at all that extreme compared to, say, Soviet pianist Emil Gilels's recording with conductor Eugen Jochum. (Gould takes just over a minute and a half longer than Gilels does.) You can even reverse Grimaud's thinking to say that the concert was a piano work played while the soloist dreams the orchestra accompaniment; every line and phrase contributing to the expansion of the piano part was heard clearly. No matter. It was hated. Passion, not clarity, was wanted. Peaks and valley, not maps. And to this day, tradition-minded listeners claim that Gould egregiously ignores Brahms's tempo markings in order to proceed at his own tortoise-like pace. Indeed, one or two determined researchers have over the years cited the markings on the composer's original manuscript as evidence for Gould's obsessive ritardandos.

Yet you can't escape the sense there are more questions to be asked. To what degree was the whole event an act, a set-up by two great performers enjoying their freedom to spice up yet another collaboration? Bernstein was an old smoothie when it came to pre-concert talks, his resonant baritone framing the work so that it would be understood in just the right context. Did Bernstein's introduction goad Gould to go even slower?

The modern concerto was invented in part by C.P.E. Bach, J.S. Bach's second surviving son and fifth child. As a musical form it grew in popularity in European concert halls during the years Napoleon was conquering much of Europe. Like any military campaign, the concerto is constructed for full theatrical effect. Gould hated the competitive side of the music business, and the concerto creates a context for competition. (At this point I'm reminded of NFL football, in which the star quarterback and the rest of the team are meant to be in cahoots even while the glamorous bazillionaire star quarterback gets all the publicity. Gould got all the publicity but was uneasy about it.)

And then there's one other fallout from the Gould-Bernstein foofaraw, concerning the near-universal vitriolic critical response to the performance. Winthrop Sargeant, in the *New Yorker*, said being there that night was akin to "riding in a delayed commuter train," never certain when one was getting home. The *New York Times*'s Harold C. Schonberg produced a clumsy fictional give-and-take between two supposedly interested parties over the concert, which suggested "maybe his [Gould's] technique is not so good." *Herald Tribune* critic Paul Henry Lang blasted the conductor, saying he had "violated elementary obligations of professional conduct" by letting Gould, now obviously "unfit for public appearances," get away with what he got away with. (Bernstein's job, in Lang's view, was to deliver the old warhorses as they were intended, Bernstein being part of the storied list of New York Phil musical directors going back to Boulez, Toscanini, Mengelberg, and Mahler.)

Lang, Sargeant, and Schonberg — plus Irving Kolodin in *Saturday Review*, among others — were heavy hitters in the critical game. Many went on to write books respected in academic as well as popular circles. One-of-a-kind, Gould-like performers were not foreign to them: outrage of one sort or another was built into music history. Yet they weren't merely unwilling to accept Gould's approach: they were offended by it. How dare he do this to Brahms? How dare he do this to anyone? How dare he...?

Gould was about to show them how — by quitting in just two years. Maybe he showed them something else: that their day was over. In other fields criticism was becoming an increasingly vital part of journalism, particularly with film and rock criticism and the emergence of critics such as Pauline Kael who used a new critical language. Classical music criticism had reached a cul-de-sac, unable to go anywhere but back from where it had come. Rock critics were worming their way into the national press. Pretty soon a review of any Beatles album would blow away the need for the coverage of any new Glenn Gould album. Oh, classical critics continued to be hired by the print medium, but by the 1970s these hires, once considered terribly prestigious, were dwindling. After 2000, specialty classical music websites have pretty much taken over and, as a result, increased the diversity of opinion. Having just written this, I go to Google and within seconds find a long, well-researched piece in defence of Gould's approach and, indeed, how he was respecting Brahms's intention.

Yet Gould paved his own way to the critical meltdown. There was an increasingly loose-cannon aspect to his life beyond performance in the late fifties and early sixties. In 1961 Gould, cellist Leonard Rose, and violinist Oscar Shumsky were named jointly as the heads of the Stratford Festival's musical activities, which were considerable in the early years of the Ontario event. Gould's very presence boosted ticket sales, and the concerts — going heavy on Richard Strauss, not to everyone's liking — were well attended. For a while it seemed the festival might become Gould's sinecure: he was forever bustling about, lecturing, writing, meeting, greeting, and giving interviews. Instead, it became his battleground. His turning a performance of Bach into a critique of audience behaviour led another musician to write that Gould should "grow up." Complaining aloud that he felt tired at another concert, he was told by audience members that they were tired of him.

CD 318

About a year before his Brahms First, Gould recorded his twelfth LP for Columbia, Beethoven's *Concerto for Piano and Orchestra No. 4 in G Major, Op. 58,* with Bernstein leading the Philharmonic. A photo of the two by Richard Avedon taken during the session shows Bernstein, in a polo sweater sitting near the piano keyboard talking as Gould, in a rumpled shirt and necktie, listened. Perhaps it should have been the other way around. Gould's return to the Fourth — he made his orchestral debut with it at age thirteen — was personal. His lyrical and reflective approach — Bernstein and the orchestra seem at times to be listening in on the soloist — reflected Gould at this period in his life while he was shedding more of the concert world's demands and excesses. His concert schedule was being honed: eighteen appearances for the 1961–62 schedule down to nine for the next season and only three for 1963–64. He refused to fly anymore, making those quick jaunts to New York all the more unlikely.

A smorgasbord of aches, pains, chronic fatigue, and a feeling of numbness in his left hand and arm were another reason for the cutbacks in Gould's schedule. He developed chronic bronchitis in his left lung while on tour — or at least he felt he did. He was delusional. He phoned his friend Peter Ostwald and told him that people were spying on him in his St. Clair Avenue apartment. Some close to him felt everything was stress-related — "hysterical, a conversion reaction," as one neurologist said — due in part to a serious (in Gould's mind) but mysterious (to others' way of thinking) altercation Gould had in 1959 at Steinway Hall on West 57th Street in New York.

William Hupfer, the company's chief technician, in a gesture of bonhomie, put his hand on Gould's shoulder in a "how-are-you" gesture. Was Hupfer, a beefy guy, far too heavy handed with Gould? Or had Hupfer broken Gould protocol and actually touched the pianist? Any clear answer was lost in the flurry of complaints back and forth. Gould, now feeling considerable pain on his left side, began legal action against Steinway for $750,000.

Gould, at the height of his fame, had Columbia Records on his side. The patrician Schuyler Chapin, the new head of Masterworks, taking over from David Oppenheim, was well on his way in his career, which would take him to be New York City's leading arts administrator and a mentor to Bernstein and later the head of the Metropolitan Opera, and then dean of Columbia University's school of the arts. Chapin brokered the deal with the piano giant, although he could easily have forced Steinway to pay through the nose. The suit was finally settled in August 1961, with the company agreeing to pay the pianist $9,372.35 for medical and legal expenses.

By that time, Gould's thoughts were elsewhere — on his battered old 318. To hard-core Gould fans, the number has totemic significance as Gould's favourite piano, his Steinway CD 318. Already road-weary and worn when he first laid eyes on it in 1960 backstage at Eaton Auditorium, the pianist loved its battered look and frisky touch. It was like his old Chickering back at the cottage, a piano that had quite a bit of harpsichord in its sound and soul. But CD 318 was old.

In 1971, as the instrument was being shipped from Cleveland to Toronto, it was dropped as it was being unloaded at Eaton's. (Gould had cancelled the Cleveland recording session.) Verne Edquist, Gould's piano technician in Toronto, said he found something wrong when he tried to tune it: there was a break in the piano's cast-iron plate, the interior harp-like metal piece strong enough to sustain the tension needed by the piano strings. Like a car with a twisted frame after an accident, it could never really be repaired. Following years of attempted fixes, Gould finally abandoned CD 318 in favour of Yamaha pianos such as the one he recorded his second *Goldberg Variations* on.

At least that's one version of the story. "And it's not true, it's simply not true," says Franz Mohr. As Steinway's lead concert piano technician from 1965 to 1992, the German-born Mohr took over from Hupfer; Gould was the first musician he worked with in America, travelling to Toronto on a near-monthly basis, falling into the Gould routine of working late and dining even later (Mohr's book, *My Life with the Great Pianists*, was published in 1996). But Gould grew increasingly frustrated due to Mohr's inability to fix CD 318.

"The plate was never broken, never," Mohr insisted as we sat in his Long Island living room brimming with mementos. Gould, in effect, was finished with Steinway and was looking at other brands.

"Glenn, I just have to put new hammers in," Mohr told him. "I will select the hammers myself. I will guarantee you will have the same touch."

"You have to promise you'll do it yourself," Gould insisted.

"But you know. I couldn't do it. I was too busy with Rubinstein and others. Steinway said they'd send the information I had to their head technicians. But by then Glenn was interested in Yamahas."

The CFII Yamaha Concert Grand Piano, the instrument Gould used to record his last four albums, including the 1981 *Goldberg Variations*, was restored by Yamaha Canada in 2012 following its many years on display in Roy Thomson Hall.

CHAPTER FOUR

The Biggest Chill

THE LANDSCAPE ARTIST

Glenn Gold was born on September 25, 1932, at 32 Southwood Drive, in the Beaches area of Toronto, to Russell Herbert ("Bert") Gold and Flora Emma Greig Gold. Bert was twenty-three and Flora thirty-four when they married on October 31, 1925. Glenn's arrival seven years later, when Flora was in her forties, was either a surprise to his parents or an example of their determination — or a bit of both. I'll go with determination. Single-mindedness animated the mother-and-son relationship for the rest of their days. And it drove Glenn to distraction. Flora had had several miscarriages prior to his arrival, so he was both a joy and a concern. While raising him she managed to insinuate into his thinking a life-long fear for his health. *Sit up straight. Stay away from crowds. Wash your hands. Watch for germs.*

As for the change of name from "Gold" to "Gould," city records show that the Beaches house was in the name of R.H. Gold into the late 1930s, when Bert changed the family's name — and Glenn's — to the less Jewish-sounding Gould. The name-change issue remains very much alive among the Gould faithful on a number of websites, with some asserting the Goulds were never Golds, and one or two others pointing out that the name Gould in itself sounds sufficiently Jewish to make the entire argument about Bert's motives moot.

Orillia Streets in Winter, painting by Arthur Shilling (oil on masonite, 1976, 24 x 18 in.).

Widespread anti-Semitism in Toronto, exacerbated by the approach of war, would have been a leading factor in Bert's actions. The city's success-ful Jewish families, the Mirvishes, Latners, Shopsowitzes, Snidermans, and others were establishing their businesses, though on the periphery of mainstream Toronto city life. Jewish doctors were yet to be hired by Toronto General Hospital, though it might bring in a single Jewish intern. In a 1946 Gallup poll only the Japanese were described as being less desirable than Jews. So being a Gould in downtown WASP Toronto had its advantages or, rather, it lacked being a Gold's disadvantages. Flora, in particular, was happy to be a Gould. Glenn, who worked in a music business distinguished by its Jewish presence, later joked that he was only Jewish during wartime.

Gold Standard Furs had its main office at 33 Melinda Street in downtown Toronto. Right next door was the *Toronto Telegram*, the stentorian voice of British royalty, Canadian conservatism, and business. Bay Street, not yet the country's financial hub, was a short walk away. Despite stories to the contrary, the young Gould took some pleasure in his father's importance in the world of business and understood how it was part of his success, as his mother reminded him.

"I remember rushing up the stairs, the two of us, to a window at the back of the house," says Clarence Doolittle, one of Gould's friends from the family's cottage. "He said, 'Look, there it is, that's where Dad works,' while pointing to a light he could see downtown. It was quite special with him." The *Telegram*, by the way, would soon move west in the city and then slip into the annals of history; sensing a reduction in readership and a quick buck to be made, the *Tely*'s owners caved in to the more successful *Toronto Evening Star*, the Liberals' champion and Glenn Gould's favourite paper, and folded up shop, tossing hundreds of journalists — myself included — out on the street. Hell, why not? Toronto was becoming a liberal city anyway.

Glenn's father, Bert, was born in Uxbridge, Ontario; it's where he met Flora. His grandfather Isaac Gold, a Methodist minister, was responsible for moving the family into the area in the first place. But Bert's father, Thomas, was one of those younger chaps who saw beyond small-town confines and commuted by train to Toronto, where the family had moved its fur business. He died in Uxbridge in 1953. Bruce, Bert's older brother, likewise stayed put, opening an appliance business in Uxbridge. Grant Gould, another brother, studied medicine, eventually practising in Vancouver. Uxbridge heard Glenn Gould's debut. The program distributed at the thirtieth anniversary meeting of the bible class of the local businessmen's organization on June 5, 1938, included the following: "Vocal Duet — Mr. and Mrs. R.H. Gold, 5-year-old Master Glenn Gold at the Piano."

Flora's family was originally from Mount Forest, a good day's journey by car, not horse, to the west. As a "Greig," Flora had reason to trace her lineage to famed Norwegian composer Edvard Grieg by way of Scotland and various Scots Greigs. These Greigs, on settling in Norway, reversed the middle vowels in the family name to "ie" to better help the locals pronounce the name. Flora's branch of the far-flung family settled in the Hamilton area, west of Toronto, in the 1830s. The Edvard Grieg–Glenn Gould connection, however distant, also helped Flora explain her own passion for music and her son's out-of-nowhere musical talent, which advanced at a prodigious pace that far exceeded her wildest dreams.

Glenn, who performed Grieg over the years, seemed curiously ambivalent about his connection to the composer, arguably best known for the *Peer Gynt Suite No. 1*. That said, Edvard Grieg was an accomplished pianist. His Piano Concerto in A minor, Op. 16, written when he was only twenty-four, remains among the most performed of all concertos.

Family values still had deep roots in small-town Ontario when Glenn Gould was a child. The provincial Conservative — and by 1942, Progressive Conservative — Party generally won elections in every town. Each town also had a bible study group, a constant in Gould's early life. One can understand why, later on, Gould tended to admire so-called conservative politicians — Richard Nixon over John F. Kennedy, for instance.

Change was also a constant well before the Goulds ever left Uxbridge. A back-country drive in just about any direction will take you past small graveyards left behind by a small Irish-Catholic community or Dutch Anabaptists, with a circle of weathered, chalk-coloured headstones in a circle facing a country road. Towns with old Scottish names like Duntroon, Dunedin, and Glenedin are near an entire township with Spanish names. In this context, name-hanging was also common: one finds some Golds, staunch Protestants, becoming Goulds, still staunch Protestants. For years there's been another Gould clan in Uxbridge, "unrelated in any way" to Bert's people, as I was informed by a curator at the Uxbridge-Scott Museum. These Goulds traced their roots back to the mid-1880s;

in 1884, one Joseph Gould began a woollen mill operation that was so successful he ended up being elected to the Legislative Council of the Province of Ontario. But earlier, Joseph's family were Golds — until one of the younger family members demanded the family become Goulds simply because it sounded more modern.

Being close to family was paramount among the reasons behind Bert and Flora's decision to buy a summer cottage at Uptergrove, a blink-and-you miss-it side-road corner going west off the main highway running north to Orillia. Besides, Bert was good with his hands at fixing up things. By putting in a furnace and heating system he made what was a summer place available for year-round living. Bert's business factored in as well. Now he was able to reach customers in the area buying his furs. Indeed, older folks around the area remember Bert driving around, his car "stuffed with furs" as he went from one store to another. This sight could only have whetted Glenn's animal-protection sentiments. He eventually even convinced his father to stop fishing, or at least to throw back what he caught. Merely thinking of perch or bass wriggling helplessly on a hook increased Glenn's desire to make it up to animals later on, one result being that half of his estate's donation went to the Toronto Humane Society, with the other half going to the Salvation Army. However, it's doubtful if he thought much about the irony of his father doing business with furs in an area first occupied by First Nations trappers and hunters — until they were given the boot by white settlers and their government.

THE SHANG

In commuting between Toronto and Lake Simcoe cottage country, the Goulds were among the new, young urbanites whose pilgrimage to their water-side vacation spots was inevitably described as "going north," although a few hundred kilometres north of Toronto is hardly the Canadian North.

In his late letters, Gould revealed his interest in Henry David Thoreau and the idyllic Walden Pond; he had plans for a radio special on Thoreau to follow his *Solitude* series. The perfect society described in *The Last Puritan*

Nicky takes his master on a bike ride.

by George Santayana is often cited as another influence on his fondness for the wilderness. But Lake Simcoe cottage country was no wilderness when he was growing up; nor was Uptergrove any Walden. In Gould's time, once-tranquil inlets, bays, and lakes came alive with the razz from outboard motors — his own included — and the droning of low-flying sea planes and all the hooting and hollering from swimmers splashing around, as more and more cottage country "opened up" in the late forties and early fifties and more and more cars headed north to the narrows between Lake

Up a stump.

Simcoe and Lake Couchiching, just past the Goulds' cottage. Blasts of big band swing ricocheting from car radios would soon be replaced by rock 'n' roll. On a clear night, anyone standing in front of the Gould place could see the glowing lights of Barrie to the west.

Long before this, though, the Group of Seven painted the blasted and gutted forests found in the massive industrial deforestation around the Georgian Bay area. Tom Thomson's *The Drive* (1916–17) suggests both a rush of water and of progress. His iconic Canadian painting *The West Wind* (1917) depicts nearly hopeless defiance — a lonely pine bent in the wind, clinging to scrubby rocks. To think that going to cottage country was, for city slickers, a trip into an innocent, unspoiled past was another urban fantasy. No wonder Stephen Leacock endlessly satirized the city slicker's prevailing view of backward small towns nestled in rural paradises. In his *Arcadian Adventures with the Idle Rich* (1914), published two years after his bestselling *Sunshine Sketches of a Little Town*, we find "the highly popular Reverend Edward Fareforth Furlong," whose "theological system" was entirely without anything "that need have occasioned in any of his congregation a moment's discomfort."

Gould himself sought out the bright lights of Orillia. Find the right person who knew him back when and you're sure to hear about Glenn Gould driving to the Seto family's Shangri-La restaurant in Orillia — "the Shang" — and having a steak and rolls with gobs of extra butter. He loved driving around the area, as he loved boating on its lakes. Another story I picked up tells about the afternoon he headed out to drive to the

*G*LENN GOULD AND *Gordon Lightfoot lived in two different worlds. But they shared the same small town growing up: Orillia, the Mariposa of Stephen Leacock's* Sunshine Sketches of a Little Town. *Some six years separated Gould and Lightfoot. But they had much in common. Like Gould, the younger Lightfoot was supported by a benign father and encouraged by a resolute mother — "my biggest fan," Gordon calls her.*

"We knew Glenn had come to town to … go to the Shangri-La, with [owner] Bill Seto and the best Chinese food," says Lightfoot. "Later, of course, I knew who he was."

Gould never really left Orillia, wanting to record at the Opera House not long before his death.

Orillia never left Lightfoot.

To visit Gould's Orillia — which he remained reluctant to talk about — you need only hear Lightfoot's descriptions of town life and the surroundings: of hiking in the woods; of pussywillows and shivering, quivering in the early spring rain; of hunting morels with the family; of a big harvest moon. All the images and impressions are "just a background, a backdrop for the concept you're working with."

Then there's the water — the lakes, inlets, bays, and narrows to be found everywhere. While Gould was heading his little power boat into choppy Lake Simcoe water, Lightfoot was "sailing my little Sunfish [sailboat] out on Lake Couchiching and getting tangled in the weeds."

"Our paths must have crossed but we never met," says Lightfoot.

nearby cottage of his former teacher, Alberto Guerrero, only to end up in a ditch. While pitching in to the communal effort to haul out the car, Gould had a door slammed on his hand, with remarkably little complaint from him.

Even when he was a kid, cottage country to Glenn meant hearing the New York Philharmonic broadcasts on wintry Sunday afternoons as the family drove south to the city. Beethoven would never sound as good again, he said.

Years later, when he wanted to get out of town, he'd get in the car and drive north, extending his trip to the cottage by many hundreds of kilometres, usually following a route that hugged close to Georgian Bay — he was fond of Manitoulin Island — or going farther, Lake Superior way, to Marathon or Wawa. But to Gould, the cottage and Lake Simcoe had a much deeper meaning than getting out of town.

LE GRAND MEAULNES

Going back to Uptergrove over a year or two to talk to people who knew him as a child, I emerge with things said that bounce off things remembered from what I've read about him and the cottage.

He was happiest in the water …

He was like a fish.

On his boat, he'd drive, his hand waving in the air. I guess he was conducting. (Bert Gould)

He was never happier than when on the water with his boat and his dog Nick in charge of the front deck.

But he'd never go on that diving board. It had a spring on it. (Neighbour Clarence Doolittle)

You could easily get your feet off of it.

He was fearless on that that boat, buzzing past the fishermen, getting them pissed off …

But not on that diving board.

The boys: *Go get on it. Come on, Glenn. Try it. Take a dive. Awwwww, Glenn, it won't bite you.*
Glenn: *No. Not me.*

Cottages change character and their meaning in the evening. They feel more comfortable in the evenings. The older places, their screen doors slammed shut for one last time that day, settle down like the old folks playing rummy in their regular places at the table, the parents with their Perry Mason paperbacks or Scotch.

Glenn: *I was my happiest in the water.*
… like a fish …
Never out of the water.
Flora Gould: *If you don't get out of the water now, we're going to cancel your practice time. It's getting late. Glenn, I mean it. Now!*
And get out of that wet bathing suit.

Familiar too is what you might see outside as the last light fades, the ritual of the way you might look at things, the little dots of house lights now visible from across the way, the water always darker and scarier than it ever was during the day, the dark outline of the landscape never exactly what you remembered either. Sound now seems to emerge from the landscape, not something inflicted on it, that glutinous sound of water under a dock, insects and frogs and loons soloing and the distant sound of cars heading through the narrows, the last outboards choked down to a low sputter and then turned off so as not to disturb the neighbours.

They'd be entirely quiet if it weren't for the piano playing. Evening was his favourite time to practise. A couple in a canoe turn left from their plans to head out of the little bay, and row back to the middle to listen. As if on cue, the rock 'n' roll from the distant cars disappears.

Mrs. Milligan (to the kids roughhousing upstairs): *Shush. You shush now down there. And listen. He's practising.*
    Shush.
    Shush. It's Bach now.

Cottages these days can be as big as suburban houses with multiple floors and windows the size of barn doors through which, at night, blinking lights from tech devices turn what should be a cozy kitchen into the cockpit of a 747. The very word *cottage* now seems quaint, like a reference in an old English novel. Once the very idea of cottage signalled something quite modest on the social scale, something middle class or blue collar. Cottages were small. The old Gould place was bigger than many, but even with further renovations done to it in recent years it is still a cottage. The space, only metres from the water to the north, from neighbours on both sides, and the woods all around, is cottage space, functionally intimate next to the great outdoors. For a kid like Glenn Gould in the 1930s, this meant you could go from fooling around in the water to fooling around in a different sort of way in the forest to fooling around on the roads. For anyone older, the cottage in its simple ways is a reminder that a kind of magic is graspable.

Fishing, no, not so much … he hated it when his father fished. Made him throw them back.
    I suddenly saw this entirely from the fish's point of view.
    … he wouldn't swat a mosquito standing right there on his own…. He was covered in mercurochrome, all those coloured dots, like a painting.
    … I am a skunk. A skunk am I. Skunking is all I know …
    Glenn was so skinny you could practically see his bones —
    His mother worried. Too much.
    He practised too much.
    He didn't practise enough.
    Flora Gould: *I can't tell you the sacrifices we've made for him.*
    We biked everywhere. His favourite competition was to see who went the least distance staying on his bike the longest. He could do five minutes.

Escape on Lake Simcoe.

He wanted to be Sam Snead.

It was always Mr. and Mrs. Gould. But they were friendly. Mothers soon knew who ate what, and we were all in and out of each other's houses.

The girls: They were here from the city. They'd be here for one, two weeks, then back to Toronto. I never saw Glenn with a girlfriend, though.

Angela Addison: *Glenn was now playing Chopin, a sop, for me, as he disliked the composer's work at the time and I walked back into the living room where I sat listening emotionally until he finished.*

Sex is in the distance as the cars rush to and from Orillia, their radios cranked up, chips and cokes, hands creeping under bra straps.

Welllll, Bebop A Lula, she's my baby …

In a 1960 letter to Edith Boecker, Gould writes "on a whim I became a tenant of an estate some fifteen miles above Toronto known as Donchery. It was love at first sight."

Going on, he tallies the number of rooms, twenty-six in all, plus the swimming pool and the tennis court. He then recounts the "gigantic buying spree" on the second day of the lease — "mattress testing has been among my favourite private pastimes," he confesses — only to suddenly realize (it was the arrival of "the Pyrex dishes" that did it) that "Donchery represented a snare." Taking a sizable financial hit, Gould gets out of his lease. "I return with my tail between my legs to Lake Simcoe, which now seems quite grand enough."

There's is something of *The Great Gatsby* in all of this as I've said — maybe a contrary Canadian version of Gatsby, of wanting and achieving, but *Gatsby* still. There's the older, reflective Glenn Gould, showing up at the cottage without his parents knowing, standing by the water's edge, wanting at that moment to never be anywhere else. There's Gatsby's narrator, Nick Carraway, knowing that the American dream, out there across the water, is unreachable. There's Glenn Gould knowing he's the Canadian dream, or is thought of as such. For him, the cottage was his escape, his version of the dream, of being *the* Glenn Gould. Also in the mix here is *Le Grand Meaulnes*. *The Great Gatsby* draws on French author Alain-Fournier's enormously influential story of adolescence, which led directly to *The Magus* by John Fowles. (F. Scott Fitzgerald and Harry Crosby, the first English translator of *Le Grand Meaulnes*, inhabited the same cafés and Paris salons.) Fowles said the French novel haunted everything he wrote. Fournier's love of the girl who got away is more than equalled in its intensity by his love for the home he grew up in, in the central Cher region of France.

Gould, for most of his life, kept returning to where he'd already been. The exception was his repertoire, other than, of course, *The Goldberg Variations*. Yet in most other ways he was forever retracing his steps. Not many months before his death in 1982, he returned to the Orillia Opera House with thoughts of recording there, where he had once performed.

Finding the lights on inside, Terry Rideout, a Bell worker who was a volunteer technician at the Opera House, walked in and showed Gould around a bit. "I then had a private concert," Terry told me. "Glenn told me he was looking at several places in the area to record in."

Gould was skeptical about progress and change. He lived with his parents for more than thirty years. His loved his routine life in later years. When not at his St. Clair Avenue apartment, where he lived from 1960 on, he would most likely be found at the CBC or at his private studio in the Four Seasons Hotel. He kept the same stocks, the same lawyers at Minden Gross. Cousin Jessie Greig remained his closest confidant throughout his life. His plans for his future were rooted in the past, including a return to the concert stage at Carnegie Hall. Even his obsessions remained fixed. He would repeatedly and obsessively phone the same person over a period of time: one woman working at Columbia Records' Canadian headquarters in Toronto in the 1970s found she had to "make excuses" to avoid his incessant calls late in the afternoon. But there was no greater constant through most of his early life than the Gould family cottage.

By the early sixties, Clarence Doolittle had married and moved to Orillia. Every so often he'd phone his mom back in Uptergrove, where the Goulds' cottage was located, and sometimes she'd say: "And, oh, I almost forgot, but Glenn has been up here for a bit."

PETULA

Gould talked for years about a nightmare that haunted him as a child, in which the landscape around his Uptergrove cottage — the trees, grass, everything — turned barren, leaving just bare boulders and dried leaves blowing in the wind. He thought and thought about it over the years, deciding that it represented his fear of returning to school or, in a broader sense, to life in Toronto.

What struck me about the rendition of the dream he taped for the CBC documentary team in 1959 was the filmic nature of the description, how he zoomed in on certain images and then drew back for a long shot.

Landscape is an idea that, on its own, is rarely associated with Gould, beyond his lifelong thinking about the North and his few swipes at the suburbs, the south, New York, and a few other cities, with which he'd spice up any script or essay — a fair amount of landscape thinking, actually. Yet few musical artists carry about them a sense of being in place as much as Gould. He rarely commented on or wrote about the visual arts, except maybe for a passing reference or two to the Group of Seven. In talking to a number of visual arts commentators — among them Roald Nasgaard, the recognized authority on Canadian abstraction — I found they mostly remembered their musical experience of Gould, their pleasure in listening to him, but not any particular influence he may have had on their area of study. Which is strange, I think, and also, perhaps, calculated.

The years Gould spent in Toronto from the mid-sixties on, after his touring days were over, saw some of the most exciting and far-reaching developments ever in the city's art scene. These were led in part by Michael Snow and other artist/musicians whose extraordinary music/sound/noise explorations could not be ignored. Snow's *Wavelength* in 1967 caused a sensation across the visual and sound arts. Other sound art transformations were happening by way of the University of Toronto's electronic music studio, the Ten Centuries Concerts, A Space Gallery, and late-night free-form rock 'n' roll radio. Gould, increasingly a CBC contributor, was seemingly not part of it. But he was. Reading his essays from the period, listening to his radio work, or watching his TV broadcasts, you sense how Gould felt he was living through an "age of flux," as he described Richard Strauss's time in *Richard Strauss: A Personal View*. (This was a CBC TV *Festival* production originally broadcast October 15, 1962; Gould was accompanied by soprano Lois Marshall and violinist Oscar Shumsky.) Gould saw himself as a *fin-de-siècle* figure, straddling eras, a witness to the dying era's confusion and decay. The most interesting program among the CBC broadcasts, which range from 1954 to 1977, is *Duo,* broadcast May 18, 1966, with Yehudi Menuhin. When the violinist goes off script (one written by Gould, of course) on the subject of Beethoven's Sonata for Piano and Violin No. 10 in G major, Op. 96, a real, spontaneous dialogue immediately breaks out between Menuhin and Gould — much to Gould's displeasure at his sudden lack of control.

Gould's vision, his way of looking at things, has that particular controlled Canadian chill that runs through much of the CBC Radio *Ideas* series and is reminiscent of a chilly Alex Colville seascape. Everything is so in-its-place, so frozen in space that it's suspicious and even deeply disturbing, like a crime scene scrubbed clean of evidence. (Colville was one of the neatest individuals I ever met, impeccably dressed during our interview in a spotless living room in Wolfville, Nova Scotia, dominated by a new Sharpe digital TV.)

Gould had remarkably perceptive views of certain aspects of landscape and the idea of landscape. Talking with *Rolling Stone* interviewer Jonathan Cott one midsummer evening in August about Strindberg's play *Miss Julie,* Gould says, "Implicit in the structure of the play, which is a very tight structure, is the notion of light — light as it happens, light that barely goes below the horizon and never altogether loses its powers and which in the end is much stronger than when the play opened."

The central character in *The Three-Cornered World,* Natsume Soseki's novel from 1906, and a Gould favourite, is a landscape painter who feels he can better observe the world the less he is a part of it. (One Soseki reference rarely noted by scholars is the joyful realization by the artist as he sets out on a new journey that "fortunately I had already left the triteness of falling in love far behind me.")

Gould's thinking about the landscape came into his radio and TV work well before he began work on *The Solitude Trilogy. The Art of Glenn Gould,* some twenty-four shows that aired between 1966 and 1967, showed Gould thinking well beyond music, with guests such as Norman McLaren, the avant-garde filmmaker, and John Diefenbaker, the former Canadian prime minister. The CBC was beginning to see Gould in a new and compelling light, as more than a recording star: as an intellectual with

Strollin' beaches style.

a home-grown media persona. The radio program *Ideas,* which began in 1965, went further and recognized Gould's growing talent as a producer. Gould eased into his new role as an *Ideas* contributor with *The Psychology of Improvisation*, broadcast late in 1966, which studied the role in music of spontaneity and improvisation. It was followed by *The Search for "Pet" Clark* (December 11, 1967).

By the late sixties it seemed that Gould had two disparate media personas. On radio, he was the polymath intellectual and CBC wit. On TV, Gould was still seen primarily as a performer, as in *Conversations with Glenn Gould*, a 1966 CBC-BBC co-production with interviewer Humphrey Burton. American TV saw the greater potential in him as a comic classical music snob/oddball, along the lines of Oscar Levant, a regular on *The Tonight Show Starring Johnny Carson* and a pianist who once had real chops, as is suggested by his performance in the film *An American in Paris*. Typically, Gould didn't reject the idea. He'd do it but he wanted control.

The Search for "Pet" Clark is seen by some as a warm-up to 1967's *The Idea of North*. After all, doesn't *The Idea of North* sound like a far more

On a rocky spit.

prestigious undertaking than a documentary of a lonely star pianist's fantasies about a British pop artist, one he never met? Maybe not. With *Search*, Gould places himself in the Canadian landscape and judges it as it judges him through his narrative device of a long and lonely car trip up Highway 17 to Marathon, near Lake Superior.

In fact, Petula Clark is not the real object of Gould's search. He'd already found her, tuning her in with his car radio as she sang "Downtown" in her unmannered, heartfelt, Teen Queen voice, "pop music's most per-suasive embodiment of the *Gidget* syndrome," as Gould says snootily on the show. (*Search* is Gould at his snooty best — and pop-cultural savviest. *Gidget* syndrome, eh?) Gould adored the linear clarity of Clark's singing while giving all due credit to Tony Hatch, Clark's producer and the song's composer. *Search* encapsulated Gould's search for pop itself: this may have been the selling point for the show in the first place. ("Gould Goes Pop" might have been the sales pitch to CBC brass.)

Gould's "analysis" of the Beatles, murky at best, reveals how much he *didn't* understand the Beatles or the quickly modernizing workings of the recording studio. What Gould didn't like about the Beatles — the

135

PETULA CLARK THOUGHT Glenn Gould was joking in the piece she read where he called her "pop music's most persuasive embodiment of the Gidget syndrome." Like, who was this fellow? Wasn't she the major pop star in 1967 when Gould's The Search for "Pet" Clark was heard on CBC radio and appeared in print in High Fidelity Musical America?

"At first I wondered what all of this was about," she says. "I thought: Is it some kind of joke? It's kind of tongue-in-cheek, I know. But then I realized. There is a kind of longing in it too."

Gould was alone as he listened to her sing "Who Am I?" on the car radio as he headed west along Highway 17 in northern Ontario, before booking into a motel room in Marathon. His critical faculties were on full alert, as when he talks about her voice being "fiercely loyal to its one great octave." But not his heart. He wasn't searching for Pet Clark. He'd found her.

"But I never ever met him," she goes on. "I wish I could have. I've seen films about him. And I've been in Canada over the years. But our paths never crossed. Much later I did a CD where I did a lyric to Bach's Sleepers Awake (Wachet Auf) and it had a very strange feeling to it, as if Bach was breathing down my neck. Or maybe it was Glenn. I feel it's all very sad."

When she's alone and life is making her lonely, Petula Clark likes to stretch out and listen to the Glenn Gould Goldberg Variations.

"We've all been there, haven't we, alone in a hotel room?"

way in which their voices were buried in each single's entire spectrum of sound — was in fact at the heart of rock sound mixing and the importance of the studio in it. Gould saw the studio as another sanctuary where he could work monk-like on the niceties of editing. Unlike George Martin, producer of the Beatles, Gould didn't really see the studio as an instrument itself — although that was the way he was being recorded by Columbia Masterworks.

Search gave Gould the chance to work with Lorne Tulk and to resurrect a professional relationship going back to the early fifties at the CBC. The CBC paired Gould with a good many bright young staff producers, like David Jaeger. But Tulk — probably Gould's closest friend and ally at the CBC — would be able to shape Gould's idea for *The Idea of North*.

WHEN THE SUN IS DOWN

Ideas producer Janet Somerville had asked Gould to create something to help celebrate Canada's Centennial in 1967, something as breathtaking and expansive as the country itself, something a visionary like Gould might create. But Gould had another idea, reflecting his interior view of the great Canadian North. As a resource he could draw on his experiences and contacts among a group of strangers heading north by train to Churchill, Manitoba, in 1965. Landscape painting and photography can convey a symphonic scope, and they have the power of the image to allude to what's beyond the frame — the vaster, unseen landscape out there. Gould's *Idea of North* was about inside — individual feeling — resulting from a process determined by interiors, by Gould locking himself away in a recording studio and sifting through hours of interviews. Gould created conversation as chamber music. Six character types are heading north: a nurse, a sociologist, an anthropologist, a prospector, a bureaucrat, and a surveyor (replace *North* with *Mars*, and you have the cast for several dozen Hollywood movies). Each character has an attitude about the North: the nurse always positive about her possibilities, the surveyor less hopeful with each passing year. In the background, there's the sound of a train rushing through the night.

Gould and Tulk treated the voices Gould taped for each chapter of *The Solitude Trilogy* in which *North* appeared "as though they belonged to characters in a play, though all the material was gained from interviews," Tulk says. "It was documentary material, treated in a sense as drama."

The television version of *The Idea of North* is much better at conveying the human context — the drinks poured, cigarette smoke, sweat, heavy clothing. You get no sense of a beckoning horizon on the radio show. It's the North like a snowy Christmas scene in a water-filled gift bubble. Swirl it around enough and see what floats. The compositional process involved in the radio production is the true successor to Gould's intricate early String Quartet, each tied up in creative knots of its own making. Whatever vision there is in *The Idea of North* "lies in the juxtaposition of perspectives, nothing more," writes critic David Howes. Then again, the North Gould wanted was truly unseeable. "Anyone can go to the Arctic Circle when the sun is up," he said, not entirely as a joke. He wanted to go "when the sun is down."

The Idea of North, Gould explained, was "an opportunity to examine that condition of solitude which is neither exclusive to the North nor the prerogative of those who go North." This condition of solitude, though, "appears ... a bit more clearly to those who have made, if only in their imagination, the journey North."

This North was actually Gould's invention for a better understanding of himself. Technology makes this possible and, better, it extends this "opportunity to examine" all the way to the sublime. "Through the ministrations of radio and the phonograph," Gould wrote, "we are rapidly and quite properly learning to appreciate the elements of aesthetic narcissism — and I use the term in its best sense — and are awakening to the challenge that each man contemplatively create his own divinity." ("Video: The Aesthetics of Narcissism," the title of an 1976 essay by American art theorist and historian Rosalind E. Krauss, centres on the idea of "the image of self-regard" defining all video art, in her time still in its formative stages.)

Gould loved the movies: he talked to me at some length about his wanting to be a director. Years later I saw him making video cinema. As a video artist he'd be entirely in synch with the hermit-like practices of other video artists, exploring and enjoying the hands-on technology. The self-centred psychology inherent in the medium makes video "the technological mirror," as Canadian video master Mike Hoolboom called it, explaining that "Gould's interest in fragmentation and collage make him a predecessor to the whole postmodernist movement."

Gould's idealized North represents "a metaphor for the sheer physical profundity of the Northern land, 'an escape from the limitations of civilization,' a state of mind," according to Anyssa Neumann in her essay "Ideas of North: Glenn Gould and the Aesthetic of the Sublime." Neumann makes it clear that she distinguishes between the geographical North and Gould's North "as a mythical, mystical or metaphysical association."

"North is an arbitrary term," wrote Charles E. Burchfield, the American landscape painter who was one of Gould's kindred souls, although they never met. (Burchfield, a Buffalo, New York, artist, would have heard Gould while listening to the CBC, which he often did.) North is a yearning, he went on. *Mystic North: Burchfield, Sibelius, & Nature,* a 2015 exhibition at Buffalo's Burchfield Penney Art Center, included a showing of *Thirty Two Short Films.* North is, in this sense, fiction, and that's how Gould meant us listeners to experience it.

The Idea of North, intended as a stand-alone show and not part of a series, was broadcast in 1967, a time when Canada was binging on east-west euphoria and naïveté — despite the separatist movement, Quebec was still with us! Everyone headed to Montreal to revel in our hundredth birthday and a collection of futuristic architecture at Expo 67. Initially, then, Gould's *North* didn't attract an extraordinary amount of attention. What followed is another story entirely.

The Idea of North has arguably attracted more comment than anything else Gould was doing at the time. It took attention away from his emerging career as a creator of film scores, starting with his 1971 soundtrack for George Roy Hill's *Slaughterhouse-Five,* based on the absurdist war novel by Kurt Vonnegut Jr., not one of Gould's favourites. As a supplier of soundtracks, he was more in synch with *The Wars,* the 1982 Canadian-made film based on the Timothy Findley novel of the same name, directed by Robin Phillips. *The Idea of North* even diverted attention away from his remarkable series of recordings through the 1970s. In the ongoing debate over Gould's *Solitude* series, one central question has been whether these works should be understood as noteless music — musical thinking applied to sound capture, editing, and audible result — or documentary arranged along lines associated with musical composition, particularly counterpoint, with one voice over another. Gould called it music and used musical terminology to describe the work.

The Latecomers, the second installment in the *Solitude* series, is more aurally suggestive/descriptive, with sounds of waves crashing into Newfoundland shorelines, after which a chorus of speakers decry the incursion of modern life into the rock-ribbed island village. *The Quiet in the Land*, the third in the series, expands the sound palette much further in its exploration of a Mennonite community by the Red River in Manitoba. Here the narrator becomes far more recognizably Glenn Gould. "When I was in Switzerland, I found people driven up in the mountains and defending why they were there historically — that they wanted to be in the world but not of it." This is the Mennonites' vision, too. But Gould is also meditating on Gould.

French musician Daniel Charles once confronted the American avant-garde composer John Cage with what he believed Cage was after. "You propose to musicate language," Charles told Cage. "You want language to be heard as music." Cage's work in this direction had mostly begun in 1939 with the electro-acoustic piece *Imaginary Landscape No. 1*, a brief work for radio with a chamber group and a prepared piano, a cymbal, and two variable-speed turntables. "I hope to let words exist, as I tried to let sound exist," said Cage.

One of Gould's most discerning listeners, Edward Said, maintained that everything the pianist did was a "continuum with the original place and time he had been afforded as a performer, the concert platform." Said wrote this in 1991, when the perspective on Gould was beginning to change and younger listeners coming to *Goldberg* for the first time were giving preferential treatment to the image of the classical hipster over that of the aging hypochondriac. Gould's (hetero)sexual life was now out in public and, to the shock of older Gould acolytes, was hardly a big deal. Everyone was catching up on the romanticized stories of Gould's midnight rides in a fat-ass, sleek Lincoln Town Car going nowhere in particular, which had just the right existential vibe. Said remarks on the contradictory nature of Gould's success: the fame he achieved later on came from his rejection of the very thing that made him famous in the first place.

Gould's evolution from player to thinker, Said also said, allowed enough space for him to be both at once. From the mid-sixties through the seventies he was recording at a furious place, even as his CBC broadcast work was taking up more of his time — recordings that contained some of his greatest performances. (Leading this list is his *Handel: Harpsichord Suites Nos. 1–4*, recorded in 1972 and released in 1984, named by one fan online as "one of the greatest recordings EVER.")

Radio offered Gould new developing technology: Ontario sound artist Gordon Monahan thinks that in itself may have been the CBC's greatest asset for Gould. But radio triggered associations and memories outside of music, associations Gould absorbed as a kid, ideas of place and time and not of the concert hall.

THE SIX

Gould might have eagerly embraced the internet, as many writers have suggested. But he already had in mind a good many TV plans stretching over the next two decades, some involving CBC producer John McGreevy, others with Bruno Monsaingeon, the French violinist and TV director who filmed Gould late in his career. One can only guess what might have resulted from Gould's growing fascination with the rapidly expanding world of TV, with pay TV, cable, and multiple channels already making new fortunes in his day.

In August and September of 1978 Gould filmed *Glenn Gould's Toronto* for John McGreevy as part of the CBC producer's international *Cities* series. Another segment of the series was *George Plimpton's New York,* and one other had Jonathan Miller poking around London. One might wonder if Toronto would have gotten the nod at all if McGreevy wasn't at the CBC and Gould wasn't the city's most internationally famous citizen this side of Marshall McLuhan and a few hockey stars. Gould loved the idea, and the pay: $20,000 plus royalties, a figure not incommensurate with his musical fees. Gould eventually turned in a script for the *Cities* series fat enough to sustain an entire series on its own. McGreevy had to trim it into shape with a critical Gould hovering over his shoulder during the months of snipping and editing.

Glenn Gould's Toronto was pretty standard fare for its day, showing us around a rather generic modern city with lots of downtown glass. Toronto might have been Frankfurt. What's fascinating, though, is what's hinted at and what's ignored completely — and why. *Glenn Gould's Toronto* is many things, but it's not Glenn Gould's Toronto. It's filled with its share of familiar Gould observations — Toronto being a city of churches, for one — and some memorable moments such as the one at Fort York with guns blasting in which the pianist seems truly startled, ducking down time and again with each volley. Along the way we find that he loathes the Eaton Centre — "it's absolutely absurd" — but is thrilled by North York's anonymous modernism. And there's that moment of wonderful, inspired silliness in which we find Gould on a misty dawn singing Gustav Mahler's *St. Anthony of Padua's Sermon to the Fish* while a pack of elephants watch with studied indifference. Conducting animals was a familiar Gould trope that survived the vicissitudes of his conducting career. One wishes it had evolved into a series.

Another wry moment comes when he explains that the CN Tower was built higher than any freestanding structure in the world so Torontonians could finally see Buffalo, New York, to the southwest over Lake Ontario. It's a good bit, smoothly executed. But his timing is off. Well before Toronto began celebrating its greatest erection, the city had outpaced Buffalo as the sexy, exciting entertainment-filled city to visit. Buffalonians now came north for their thrills; we didn't go south.

The segment suggests not so much Gould's lack of information — he was an avid newspaper reader — but the degree to which he had distanced himself from the city that Toronto had become, as he admits from the start of the program. At one juncture he notes that Yorkville, Toronto's hippie village, developed because of American draft dodgers, when in reality its population came mostly from the city's suburbs. This disconnect was played out after the finished show was about to get its public send-off at city hall, which Gould declined to attend. The no-show resulted in some of the first bad press he ever received in his own hometown, aside from the occasional negative record review. "He merely sneers at us all," wrote the *Star's* Rob Base. Still, the Gould spirit lived on with then-mayor John Sewell, aiming to bring some hope to the waiting crowd and perhaps conjure up the nocturnal Gould. "But someone said it's still daylight out," quipped Sewell, an earnest urban reformer type hardly known as a funny guy.

The absence in McGreevy's documentary of any mention of the Beaches neighbourhood — and Gould's childhood home on its northern edge, former farmland turned urban in the 1940s and 1950s as a nondescript suburb — is understandable given Gould's reticence about revealing anything of his life that he didn't control. The finest description of Gould's early life, his bland surroundings and middle-brow childhood, comes from Robert Fulford, one of Canada's leading print journalists for decades, who happened to have lived next door to Gould, at 34 Southwood Drive. (Yet another irony this, considering Gould's well-honed instinct for privacy.)

Fulford recognized early on — as did Gould's Uptergrove friends — the cost Gould had to pay along his road to stardom, including having to absorb the relentless pressure of his mother, who was "always admonishing Glenn about something," Fulford later wrote. In 1952, as we have seen, Gould and Fulford formed the New Music Associates — a precocious concert series, considering the organizers' age and inexperience — given over mostly to atonalism's new wave composers and, of course, Bach, whenever possible. Gould provided musical direction while Fulford, then a sportswriter, handled all practical matters from PR to hall rental. The series' brief existence is characterized in most music histories as not having much to do with Gould, if it is mentioned at all. But it gave Maureen Forrester her Toronto debut and provided the platform for Gould to play *The Goldberg Variations* in public for the first time. One guesses that Fulford might have been Gould's official biographer later on had they not eventually fallen out, a not uncommon turn of events for many of Gould's early friendships.

Fulford's writing about Gould and their Toronto goes in a different direction from Gould's. What Fulford loathes about the early days, Gould remembers fondly, wishing things had been left unchanged. There was "tranquility in the city only if one opted not to be a part of it," Gould reminisced for McGreevy. In condemning the city's "closed, deadening WASP world," Fulford tapped into a long and distinguished tradition of Toronto-bashing that was mined night after night by burlesque comics and the like who "had" to play Toronto. The leading Toronto critic of his own day was Ernest Hemingway during his (miserable) stint as a reporter for the *Toronto Daily Star*. Why, said Hem, the best thing Torontonians had going for them was their streetcar system. He brought his wife, Hadley, to Toronto to have their first child only because having babies is "the *specialité de ville*," Hemingway ranted in a letter to Ezra Pound. "They don't do anything else."

Glenn Gould picked up the theme, although he managed to ignore the famous complaint about not being able to drink on Sunday. "I'm not really cut out for city living, and given my druthers I'd probably avoid all cities and live in the country," he says only a minute or so into *Glenn Gould's Toronto.* "Toronto, however, belongs on a very short list of cities which I've visited and which seem to offer to me, at any rate, peace of mind — cities which, for want of a better definition, do not impose their *cityness* upon you." (Leningrad [St. Petersburg] was his favourite at the time.) Later he says that that most of his memories of childhood "have to do with churches, not school" — *particularly* not school. The school week meant days of jostle and uncertainty and kids who didn't always understand the "uncommonly sensitive soul" — as Gould described himself, not entirely tongue-in-cheek — in their midst.

Sundays were controlled. The services held at evening time, his preferred time, meant more subdued ritual and music, and muted colour cast on polished wood surfaces from stained glass windows. Sunday was a "sanctuary," as he says. This is an important idea. Sanctuary was being alone at the cottage, or being alone in a car heading just about anywhere. Toronto was a sanctuary as well, at least his idea of Toronto, his ideal Toronto. The city itself, "new, brash, ragtag," as one architect put it, was bursting at its seams with immigration from Italy and Portugal renewing and revitalizing squat, old, neglected neighbourhoods. Its population reached the one-million mark in 1951. But Gould liked to keep the idea of the old WASP Toronto alive. This stolid, grey, wintry city illuminated a wintry Gould capable of making Moscow sound positively cheery by comparison.

Toronto was a valuable resource in the growing business of Gould being Gould, who loved loving a city for everything others would not. A cold, gloomy, church-ridden Toronto suited his needs as Manhattan or Queens or Brooklyn provided fodder for an old-school stand-up comedian like Henny Youngman.

(Youngman on New York: A man says to another man: "Can you tell me how to get to Central Park?" The guy says no. "All right," says the first. "I'll mug you here.")

(Gould on Lake Ontario: The least great of the Great Lakes.)

Gould sold Toronto's squareness throughout his life, and made it a civic virtue. Yet it wasn't the city's whole story, and he knew it. McGreevy's documentary shows him driving down Yonge Street, seemingly ignoring the side of Toronto that he dismissed as being the inevitable detritus of the modern urban landscape. One of the shop signs he passes (twice) was a famous Toronto neon landmark: the circling LPs denoting Sam the Record Man. As documentary film goes, this is a rather standard shot — the garish city all lit up. *Rock records: Ooooh!* But, in fact, Gould not only knew and walked down Yonge Street over the years; he developed a friendship with Sam Sniderman, the influential front man of the legendary record-store chain. (Gould's friendship with Sniderman was also protecting the Gould brand. Any musician of any stripe needed Sam the Record Man to hustle the "product.")

"He'd be in and out all the time," Sam told me not many months before his death in 2012. "Then it's Christmas or almost Christmas and we're closing up or already closed and I get the call: 'Sam, pick out some records for me,' he'd say. 'I need them for gifts.'

"'Glenn, we're closed. Besides, I'm picking out music for you?'

"'Sam, please,' he'd say. So of course I would."

DEAR FATHER

Bert Gould may still be best remembered for tailor-making his son's iconic folding wooden chair in 1953, remaining its chief repairman for years to come. I still wonder to myself: would any father know more about the ways of his boy's body than Bert would by watching Glenn fold around or perch himself in that wonky chair? There are those who think the chair did little to ease Glenn's back and shoulder problems and may indeed have been part of the cause. The chair's shape mirrored its occupant's. (Learning how to replicate Glenn's playing posture, says actor Colm Feore, gave him a better understanding of Gould's character for his role as the pianist in François Girard's *Thirty Two Short Films About Glenn Gould*.) For someone as tormented as he was with aches and pulled muscles, Gould managed to twist himself into a striking variety of positions. He chafed at his mother's forever telling him to sit up. He wouldn't alter in the slightest his nose-to-the-keyboard position, which, years along, would be blamed on the example set by his teacher, Alberto Guerrero.

Bert liked being on call to fix the damn chair. And he eventually took on the role of chief custodian of the domestic side of his son's legacy, responding to a steady stream of requests, mine included, as I was assembling a high-end coffee table book of iconic or unexpected Glenn Gould imagery for publication. From what I heard, Bert remained helpful to everyone, although with some difficulty after he and Glenn had drifted apart following Flora's death in 1975, and more specifically following Bert's marriage to Vera Dobson on January 19, 1980. One of Glenn's most famous letters is the carefully written note declining Bert's offer that Glenn be his best man at the wedding. "Dear Father — I've had the opportunity to give some thought to the matter of your wedding," Glenn wrote. It was a letter between near strangers. "Mrs. Dobson" is how Glenn referred to his new stepmother.

As Bert and I sorted through a cardboard box full of memorabilia — postcards, the usual stuff — Bert gave the impression he'd been through it all before, had seen it all before, and wasn't watching too closely.

"Why did he keep it all?" I asked at one point, holding on to two items with the same hotel logo. "It could not have been to remember where he'd been?"

I meant it as a joke, Glenn's memory having been as famous as his technique. Bert, rather formally dressed for the occasion with sports jacket and tie, took it seriously. "I think it was for us, as a way for him to remember to tell us later on," he said. "We got letters and postcards. But sometimes he'd be somewhere and come back and he'd be gone again, up to the cottage usually, and we might not even see him for days."

What I detected at the time was something missing in Bert's voice; something I expected might be there. It certainly wasn't nostalgia. I selected certain items I thought would work visually, told him I'd be back for them if the project ever found a buyer. (It didn't.) Bert seemed far more remote a figure than I expected. I knew soon enough there was much he wasn't giving away — and I don't mean matchbook covers. Many years later, one of the Gould family's Uptergrove neighbours I'd

Bahamas 1955: Gould plays director.

Bahamas 1955: Places everyone.

come to know slightly remembered the day Grant Gould, Bert's brother, dropped by to visit Bert at the cottage and was startled to hear it had been sold — four years earlier.

"He hadn't been told," said the neighbour. "Bert just moved on."

I've known a number of men of Bert's generation who closed up a summer place like that, wordlessly shutting down their connection with everything the place was and what it meant, the summer long ago and the winter evenings in the bush, closing the door, giving it a pat —feeling the cracked paint ever so slightly — checking the lock to make sure it was tight, and walking to the car leaving nothing, really, behind.

FINALE

The Magus's Mysterium

Alexina Louie was already working on a large-scale string piece in her Toronto study when she heard Glenn Gould had died. It stopped her cold. She found that "every time I tried to turn the piece back to being what it was before, it went on by its own free will to become what it wanted to be," the Toronto composer told me. "And every time I came back to the piece I started to think of Gould. At his memorial service [Toronto, 1982] we all sang *Nun danket alle Gott*, the Bach chorale. When I went back to continue writing again I wanted to include *Nun danket alle Gott* in the work. I write at the piano and I began to meditate on certain pieces by Bach and Mahler. I began to translate the sounds of the piano into the strings."

O Magnum Mysterium: In Memoriam Glenn Gould, completed in 1984, has since become one of the hits of contemporary Canadian classical music with performance worldwide. A who's who of music history, from Palestrina to Poulenc, has set the words of the chant derived from the Latin text *"O Magnum Mysterium"* from the Matins of Christmas: few have done it with the coloration brought to it by Louie.

Even so, the title still seems slightly askew. You might wonder, was there ever a less "mysterious" musician than Glenn Gould? He had a corporeal presence to those who knew him only through his music. And those mystery-making traits — his contradictions, his evasiveness, funny self-deprecations, inexplicable mood swings — define the very real, perceptible Glenn Gould.

Yet there was a kind of mystery about Glenn Gould's final years. He disappeared before he died. He disappeared as a media presence; he disappeared as a physical presence. His CBC work was dwindling, his last TV appearance coming in 1979 when he plays *Désir*, the first of Scriabin's Two Pieces, Op. 57. His last on radio came in 1981 with an appearance on the show *Booktime*, where he read parts of the initial chapter of Soseki's *The Three-Cornered World*.

His relationship with the CBC had by that point deteriorated. Old pals and mentors had left. His time-consuming need for technical perfection far outstripped the Corp's technical competence and willingness to pay union wage for all the extra hours Gould wanted to spend in the studio. He didn't seem to be in the papers or magazines anymore, either. Once you could construct your own Glenn Gould history by merely stringing together in your mind the press photos you remembered from over the years. Not anymore. Even his image had gone missing: a *magnum mysterium* indeed.

He'd gone underground, his own underground of midnight car rides to and from more and more studios and concert halls he'd hired secretively. He was in the process of reinventing himself — again — through his determination to become a conductor, an ambition dating back to the late fifties. As if that was not enough, he had plans to reinvent music on TV. The exhausting schedule he maintained in 1982, the last year of his life, included a conducting session in April in Hamilton, where he recorded two movements of Beethoven's Piano Concerto No. 2 in B-flat major, Op. 19, with a rental orchestra. Pianist Jon Klibonoff, studying at Julliard, was hired to stand in for Gould as the soloist but disagreed with Gould's leisurely interpretation. Orchestra members loved Gould's commitment but found his conducting baffling at times. The project was abandoned.

In July 1982 Gould conducted and recorded the chamber version of Wagner's *Siegfried Idyll* with fifteen musicians, many from the Toronto Symphony Orchestra, at the St. Lawrence Hall in Toronto. Critics weren't much moved when the recording was released years later, but Gould was through-the-roof with excitement, convinced his conducting career had finally begun. Inevitably, he began making lists of works to do.

Musicians he worked with at this time would years later report how poorly he had been looking then; how he'd gained weight, was rapidly growing bald, and was pasty-looking. He was arguing more but could still be as charming as ever, seemingly on close terms with everyone in the St. Lawrence Hall ensemble.

His work schedule was staggering. Between February 8 and 10, 1982, he went to RCA's Studio "A" in New York to record Brahms's 4 Ballades, Op. 10. He was back there again on June 30 and July 1 to record the Brahms Rhapsodies, Op. 79. The album was released March 1, 1983. Also released in 1983 in August was his *Beethoven Piano Sonatas — No. 12 in A-flat Major, Op. 26 / No. 13 in E-flat Major, Op. 27/1,* recorded in 1979 and August 1981 with Andrew Kazdin at Eaton Auditorium.

Earlier in 1982 he gave himself over to working on the soundtrack to *The Wars,* the Robin Phillips–directed Canadian movie based on Timothy Findley's novel. The score drew on Brahms, Bach, and Strauss, along with early hymns and First World War songs such as "Tipperary." Better yet, he became deeply involved in the sound mixing and editing process.

Glenn Gould's last solo recording came as part of an all-Strauss album that was eventually released on February 4, 1984. The work positioned second on the recording *R. Strauss: Five Piano Pieces, Op.3* had been recorded in 1979 in Toronto. The No. 1 Andante and No. 3 Largo were done at St. Lawrence Hall on April 23, 1979. The No. 2 Allegro vivace scherzando and No. 4 Allegro molto were recorded at Eaton Auditorium, August 6; the No. 5 Allegro marcatissimo was recorded September 5, also at Eaton Auditorium.

And so from September 1 to 3, 1982, Gould was in RCA's Studio "A" recording Richard Strauss's Piano Sonata in B minor, Op. 5. There'd been an earlier session for the work on July 2. Strauss had written the piece as a seventeen-year-old, and Gould sounds only too happy to channel the work's youthful exuberance. After the recording session Gould spoke to producer Sam Carter and wondered why more pianists didn't perform such obvious crowd-pleasing showpieces.

By now age was very much on Gould's mind. Approaching fast was his fiftieth birthday, on September 25, a date Gould had long talked about as the half-point in his work. Rumours of celebrations were already in the air. Columbia wanted something; Bert Gould wanted something else. Gould wanted none of it. He worried about unwanted congratulatory excesses on the part of would-be well-wishers. There'd be none of that. He was even standoffish to Bert and stepmother Vera when they showed up at his apartment with gifts: he took the cookies and knitted sweater they had for him in the parking lot. Otherwise he stayed holed up, spending hours on the phone reading his friends a *New York Times* tribute by Edward Rothstein on the second *Goldberg Variations* recording. The next day Gould called Rothstein in the late afternoon, surprising the *Times* critic at the earliness of the hour and the intimacy of the tone. It was the eve of Yom Kippur, Rothstein pointed out, a time of introspection and withdrawal; the chat would have to wait until the following Thursday. By then Glenn Gould would be in a coma.

Near mid-afternoon, Monday, September 27, Gould's assistant Ray Roberts received an anxious call from Gould from his suite at The Inn on the Park. Roberts, accustomed to a litany of ailments and miseries, knew his old friend was really rattled this time. He called Dr. John Percival, Gould's physician, who told Roberts to get Gould to a hospital immediately.

Picking him up at his suite — with the hotel staff helping to get the pianist into a wheelchair — Roberts sped to Toronto General Hospital in Gould's Lincoln. Gould, now feeling slightly better, and back in control, immediately began a round of phone calls before falling asleep. Roberts had his own calls to make. Cousin Jessie Greig rushed over, as did Bert. A stroke was suspected. Gould was unconscious as his father held his hand. Later the following night, Wednesday, he had another stroke and fell into a coma. By now the press had caught on: Columbia Records had readied a press release. On Thursday Gould needed a breathing tube, and his condition had worsened considerably. On Monday, October 4, with his father's agreement, he was taken off life support.

His memorial service later in the month at St. Paul's Anglican Church was a state funeral by any other name. Indeed, he was now public and state property. In the following years the Glenn Gould Foundation would establish the cash-generous, prestigious Glenn Gould Prize among its other activities, which include maintaining a Gould website; the Glenn Gould Estate kept his artistic legacy alive through various projects. And there have been years and years worth of Glenn Gould colloquia, critical studies, and tabloid-style revelations. His grave in Mount Pleasant Cemetery became a shrine. Tourists were offered Glenn Gould tours around Toronto. Charities benefited. In his will, Gould — who viewed making a will the equivalent of passing a self-imposed death sentence — afforded his father the interest for life in a $50,000 trust fund. He divided $750,000 between the Toronto Humane Society and the Salvation Army. Gould thought this was not his real will, but a preliminary draft. He had always planned to live to be a hundred.

BRUNO

Glenn Gould had a co-conspirator over the last ten years of his life: Bruno Monsaingeon. The French violinist, who began a promising career in the early sixties — he was still touring fifty years later — came across a Gould Bach performance recorded at a 1957 concert in Vienna while he was sifting through a stack of records in a Moscow record store in 1965. Hearing it a bit later was a near religious experience. "It was, it was …" Bruno puffed on his electronic cigarette "… incredible."

The story became a staple in every telling of the Monsaingeon-Gould relationship, yet it sounded fresh and new as he repeated it for my benefit. We were talking in his suburban Paris home located in Montrouge, a modern town south of the city.

The suburb's otherwise unremarkable daily life was shattered early in 2015 by the terrorist-related killing of a young policewoman by a murderer related to the Charlie Hebdo massacre. But that reality seemed years away the afternoons I was there: a sense of getting along was in the air. A woman returned my coat, which I'd left in a local bar the day I talked to Bruno. A cab driver quitting his shift offered me a free ride another day I talked to Monsaingeon, whose Gould translations — *Le dernier puritain* (1983), *Contrepoint à la ligne* (1985), *Non, je ne suis pas du tout un eccentrique* (1986) — have grown the pianist's reputation in a country Gould

Album shot: shoeless for the 1982 recording of *The Goldberg Variations*.

happily avoided. I took the ride but paid the bill, and I began to wonder: Why are cars inevitably involved in Glenn Gould stories?

With some TV work under his belt in the early seventies, Monsaingeon contacted Gould, who responded with an invitation to come to Toronto. They first met there in 1972. The word *conspiracy* implies a shared, secret pact. Gould and Monsaingeon had two. One was their shared determination to show music on TV in a way never before imagined. Their second, unstated, pact was based on Monsaingeon's awe-struck adoration for Gould's talent.

"This is most incredible, but it's impossible to analyze his piano playing," Monsaingeon told me. "Every musician uses dynamics for the sake of expression. Glenn's expressivity — the transcendent feeling you get from his Bach or his Brahms — is not by way of the usual methods of expression. It's all about restraint, restricted dynamics, of *not* playing forte or fortissimo. It's the integration of all different elements together, the rhythms, articulation, of using the minimum of theatrical elements like sforzandos or sudden pianissimos. His spectrum of decision is a deliberately restricted one. Freedom and rigour. They're always present in all recordings whoever the composer might be."

Les chemins de la musique, their first series of four shows, was filmed and broadcast in 1974 by the main French government channel, ORTF. The fall of 1973 was the expected due date, but Gould's shoulder problems caused delays.

"What should have been a terrible obstacle — and was indeed for the producers of these films — was a fantastic plus for us because I had time to commute to Toronto just about every month, where we wrote and changed and polished our texts and rehearsed them to the last little detail," Monsaingeon went on. "In terms of the intellectual content there was a total compactness in what we wanted to say. And he was ideal to work with in the sense that he was not a protagonist who's being filmed but an active protagonist. This is why we got along so wonderfully together. I was both a musician and a filmmaker. He was both a very great musician and somebody who knew what film was about. He had no direct competence in framing, or movement of camera or lights, and so forth. So he let me have complete freedom as far as it came to purely cinematic procedures. He was indeed very active in terms of the drama that was part of our scripts and part of our scenario. It had to do with the building of a dramatic structure of which Glenn was a part. We spent years preparing our films.

"There was, however, no script for *L'alchimiste,* the second part of *Les chemins.* It was improvised along an outline but an outline which was very strict and very controlled. We improvised our conversations. Each take was totally different. I did the editing later in Paris. *Glenn Gould Plays Bach,* the series we did next, was entirely predetermined. We'd started talking about it in 1976. We didn't finish until the last thing we did in 1981. It was *The Goldberg Variations.*"

Originally thought of as simply the fifth episode in the Bach series, Gould's plan to re-record *The Goldberg Variations* was soon recognized as something special: the master revisiting his masterpiece. Columbia Records' 30th Street Studio, about to be abandoned, was booked for the dates in April and May 1981. There was a sense of occasion.

"One of the difficulties of the filming was that film and disc recordings were taking place simultaneously, except for a few things," Monsaingeon explained. "Prior to the shooting we would talk on the phone endlessly about the choice of tempos, about the mathematical relationship between each variation. The process of recording was not reality. It was a staged reality. Every shot was done separately according to an outline that was precisely laboured over in my script. We would discuss his tempos. He wanted the film itself to have a certain rhythm. And I think he was look-ing for approval.

"We decided to make the film in New York with a crew I would recruit one by one, making sure people involved *would* be involved and not just taken for their purely technical competence. One of the great things about Glenn was that the film and the recording was a co-operative action."

Considering the autumnal atmosphere found in both the film and recorded versions of the second *Goldberg Variations,* the actual process proved to be a happy one for everyone. Gould was in particularly good spirits, kibitzing with the crew, laughing at himself when he couldn't actually fake a shot of playing when the film shooting script required only a visual of him behind the keyboard, not actually playing. There was even talk Monsaingeon went in "to make a film *about* 'the making of the recording of the *Goldbergs.*' I was not allowed to do that, because of the German producer."

"Bruno, could you see my legs?" Gould says into the mike shown in one of the used bits from the "making of" film.

"No," says Monsaingeon. "I'm sorry, but the angle was not on your legs during the shoot."

"Too bad," says Gould, "because I had my legs crossed on purpose to take the casual approach."

"Glenn was in ecstasy, yet he had his legs crossed!" Monsaingeon said, as the afternoon ticked away. "Here was the mixture of deliberation — the deliberate staging of his body movement and of his legs — when the fact was he was totally in the music. He would never discard intensity for the sake of acting. It was the double approach, as if both were present."

While he was telling me this I realized I was being slowly directed out the door and back into the quiet Montrouge street. Monsaingeon had to be in Germany within hours, which meant a dash to Charles de Gaulle Airport on the other side of Paris on his scooter, a life-threatening business needing full truck-avoiding concentration. He repeated the oft-told story of being driven by Gould in his Lincoln way past midnight after a *Goldberg* session up past Times Square, while Gould "was wearing blinkers, the way horses do, not to see things on each side," said Monsaingeon.

"I don't see Glenn as a tragic figure at all," said Monsaingeon, as I waited on the street for my taxi.

Why are cars involved in everything about Glenn Gould? I again found myself thinking.

"I see him as a jubilant artist in perfect control of what he wants to do and what he does," Monsaingeon went on. "I saw the dour, contemplative aspect of Glenn. Yes. This was a man who was able to remain in the same position for hours, just reflecting. He didn't need to have movement. He didn't need to have anybody around. That was the ambivalence about him. Here was a man who was out of the world, who did not want to be seen, who did not want to have physical contact with anyone, a man who wanted absolute isolation, but a man who, at the same time, had ideas about communication with others that were essential.

"He managed to reconcile the two, communication and isolation. He found a way of having a brotherly attitude toward his fellow man by withdrawing from the world."

CODA

The Lesson

Erika recognized him as the little motor boat she was in approached the shore. Spring had come but it was still cool.

He was already outside, she thought, almost as if he was waiting in front of his cottage. That was strange. When she called in the fall of 1961, his father had picked up the phone. Mr. Gould was very nice and suggested the best way to meet Glenn was to simply drop by the cottage on the chance he'd be there, as he so often was.

"If he's here I'm sure he'll be happy to help," Bert said.

A guy Erika knew, Patrick, said he knew the way to the Gould place by boat. It would have taken them forever to find their way by road. Time was on her mind. She was running out of it to get ready for the upcoming Kiwanis Music Festival.

"I phoned your father," she told him, getting out of the boat. "He said you could help with this piece."

He glanced at the cover. *Was that a smile?*

He would like her German accent, she thought, playing as much German music as he did. She'd bought an LP of him playing Schoenberg and Mozart at Gordon Electric in Orillia. Her stepmother talked about him, too; she was a baker, her muffins sold at the Champlain Hotel where he went to have tea some afternoons.

He looked curiously at the score she was holding close to her body to keep it from getting wet — Beethoven's Sonata No. 14 in C-sharp minor *"Quasi una fantasia": The Moonlight Sonata.*

Wintry photo shoot for Gould's *Beethoven Piano Sonatas* album.

"I'm having issues with it," she said.

Was that a smile on his face? What issues did he ever have? With anything?

She'd been impetuous with that phone call, she knew. Her expectations were way too high — and she didn't care. Playing this one piano piece — playing any piano piece — was something that had to be done, to prove to her father she could do it. Then he'd believe she at last had this little bit of talent.

Father, father. A fearsome figure looming over her entire life, violent at times; used his fists. He was born in 1912 in Cologne. She was born in nearby Rheinbach in 1944. She once went to the Beethoven-Haus in Bonn, only twenty kilometres away. But when the British and the Americans intensified their bombing as the war was winding down, father moved the family to Berlin, thinking it'd be safer. It wasn't. It was worse. Berlin was rubble. Food was scarce. There was no heat. And this was the devastation that confronted a newly impoverished family that had been given a house as a wedding present. Her mother couldn't stand it and eventually got a divorce from her father. The kids were split up for a bit, Erika, as custom would have it, going with her.

Her father immigrated to Canada in 1954 on the promise of a skilled job. Any job would do. The cultured, middle-class German life he'd come from — over the years the family had boasted medical people, an author, and an accomplished violinist, Else Freist — were destroyed by the war. All the beautiful things accumulated over the years — the silverware, the china, the polished furniture, everything — were now without value. No one could afford to buy them. The old man remained embittered for much the rest of his life that the family hadn't been able to afford to send him to university, although being a mechanic and chauffeur kept him out of the mainstream of the war and may have saved his life.

Erika was eleven when her father was able to bring his family to Canada. The Kitchener area was the original destination, but a bureaucratic mistake landed them in Orillia, where he had found work as a mechanic and a general fix-it man. Kitchener would have been better. Many Germans had moved there. In Orillia, Erika was an outsider, a strange kid with strange clothes speaking a strange language. Kids in grade seven bullied her the way they bullied the Indian kids from Rama.

The good of it was, she became great friends with Arthur Shilling, the Ojibwa artist. But there was not all that much else that was good about it. The school made her take commercial courses. Extracurricular activities were forbidden because father wanted her at home to help out in his new TV repair business. So she had no school friends, and after graduation she had to take an electronics course at a trade school. "You're too stupid to be out in the working world," her father told her. So he had her keep the business books. And repair radios. And go out on house calls with him. Music? She was dreaming, kidding herself.

So Erika just had to convince Glenn Gould, the very famous and busy Glenn Gould, to help her with her piece. She'd seen him on TV a number of times, in particular the CBC interview with him following his return from the Russian tour. Still, he was the only musician she knew of who was nearby and could do it. And she secretly knew he might. He could be funny and did oddball things, she'd heard. She'd heard of his generosity from her stepmother, who'd once given her Gould's autograph on a napkin.

His eyes lit up when he saw the title: *Beethoven.*

"I'm having issues with it," she said. "It just doesn't sound right."

"Come on," Gould said. "Let's see."

He looked hard at the score and frowned. Unable to read music, Erika had written the letter name of each note about it.

"You know, you should learn to read music," he said.

She tried the piece first.

"All right," he said. "Let me show you how it's done."

When he was through with the first movement, Gould showed her how the pedalling worked, how to hold the pedal down to keep a note going and then lift up her right foot.

"That's better," he said. "Practise it."

"To prove to myself I can play it, I'm going into the Kiwanis Music Festival," she said during a break.

"I guess it makes sense why you're doing that," he said. After all, he'd won first prize in the Kiwanis Music Festival in 1944. "If you have a bad day you're going to think you're not very good. But, if you have a good day, you'll feel better." He could be funny, vulnerable. "You'll do well."

"This is going to be my one performance only on the piano," she said. "I'm never going to play again."

Never going to play again.

Looking outward and inward.

What? It feels nervous and strange to be coming here again after all these years? It must indeed. No, don't bother to look at the reflection of your face in the window pane shadowed by the night outside. Nobody could tell you now after all these years. Your face has changed in those long years of money-getting in the city. Perhaps if you had come back now and then, just at odd times, it wouldn't have been so.

— STEPHEN LEACOCK, "L'Envoi: The Train to Mariposa" in *Sunshine Sketches of a Little Town*

THE LIFE AND TIMES OF
GLENN GOULD (1932–1982)

1932 Born in Toronto on September 25, Glenn Herbert Gold to parents Russell Herbert (Bert) and Florence (née Greig) Gold. His childhood and formative years are spent at his family home at 32 Southwood Drive in the Beaches district of Toronto. The family would change its name to Gould. Studies piano with his mother until the age of ten, and then attends the Toronto Conservatory of Music (now known as the Royal Conservatory of Music).

Spring 1940 Publishes *The Daily Woof — The Animal Paper*, all handwritten.

1940–47 Studies theory of music with the renowned Leo Smith. During 1942 to 1949 he also studies organ with Frederick C. Silvester.

1943–52 Studies piano with Alberto Guerrero. In June 1945 he passes his ATCM (Associate Toronto Conservatory of Music), when he is only twelve years old. He has the highest marks in all of Canada.

December 12, 1945 His professional debut as an organist at the Eaton Auditorium, Toronto. This same year he begins studies at Malvern Collegiate Institute Toronto. He is thirteen years old.

May 8, 1946 His debut as a soloist with the Toronto Conservatory of Music Orchestra, conducted by Ettore Mazzoleni, in the first movement of Beethoven's Piano Concerto No. 4.

January 14, 1947 Debut with the Toronto Symphony Orchestra conducted by Sir Bernard Heinz at Massey Hall. He performs the complete Piano Concerto No. 4 by Beethoven.

October 20, 1947 First public recital as a piano soloist for International Artists at the Eaton Auditorium in Toronto.

December 24, 1950 First broadcast for the CBC (Canadian Broadcasting Corporation), on *Sunday Morning Recital*. At the same time he finishes composing his Sonata for Bassoon and Piano.

October 1951 Tours western Canada; also has his debut with the Vancouver Symphony Orchestra.

September 8, 1952 Becomes first pianist to be televised by the CBC; it was the official opening of the CBC Toronto television station CBLT.

November 6, 1952 Has his Montreal debut at the Ladies' Morning Music Club at the Ritz Carlton Hotel.

1953 Makes his first commercial recording with violinist Albert Pratz for Hallmark, Toronto. Also has his first concert appearance at the Stratford Festival in Ontario. On December 23, he performs the Piano Concerto, Op. 42, by Schoenberg with the CBC Symphony Orchestra, conducted by Jean-Marie Beaudet.

January 1955 Two recital debuts: January 2 in Washington at the Phillips Gallery and January 11 in New York at the Town Hall. The day following the second recital, January 12, Gould signs an exclusive contract with Columbia Records.

June 10–16, 1955 Gould's first recording for Columbia records is Bach's *The Goldberg Variations*. A tour follows in the fall, with plays dates in Canada and the United States. This same year the Montreal String Quartet records Gould's String Quartet, Op.1, as a transcription recording for CBC International Service (now Radio Canada International).

January 26, 1957 Plays Carnegie Hall with the New York Philharmonic Orchestra directed by Leonard Bernstein, performing Beethoven's Piano Concerto No. 2.

February 20, 1957 Conducts a pick-up orchestra for the Chrysler Festival, which was televised on CBC. Maureen Forrester is the featured soloist.

1957 Embarks on his first overseas tour, playing recitals in Moscow, Vienna, and Leningrad. He appears with the Moscow Philharmonic Orchestra (May 8), the Leningrad Philharmonic Orchestra (May 18), and the Berlin Philharmonic Orchestra under the careful conducting of Herbert von Karajan (May 24–26). He now has rock star status in the Soviet Union. Worn down by this itinerary, he escapes to the family cottage at Uptergrove on Lake Simcoe.

August 25, 1958 Leaves for his second overseas tour. At the Brussels World's Fair he plays with the Hart House Orchestra of Toronto under Boyd Neel. Other tour cities include Stockholm, Berlin, Salzburg, and Florence. He performs an exhausting eleven concerts in eighteen days in Israel.

1959 Performs the first four of the five Beethoven piano concertos in London. Joseph Krips is the conductor of the London Symphony Orchestra. The Lucerne Festival on August 31 in his last European concert. While in New York, Gould feels he is injured by a technician from Steinway and Sons who gave him a solid pat on the back. Gould sues Steinway for $750,000; they settle out of court for a lesser amount. The National Film Board produces *Glenn Gould: Off the Record* and *Glenn Gould: On the Record*. The Symphonia String Quartet records Gould's String Quartet, Op. 1.

1960 His American television debut, performing with the New York Philharmonic under Leonard Bernstein (January 31). He also performs a Gala Performance for the Orchestra Fund with the Montreal Symphony Orchestra in Montreal on April 19. He makes three appearances at the Vancouver International Festival on July 27 and 29, and August 2.

1961 The Stratford Festival hires Gould as co-director of music with Stratford musical veterans cellist Leonard Rose and violinist Oscar Shumsky. Gould gains fame as a television commentator as well as a television performer. The CBC TV program *The Subject Is Beethoven* is a collaboration with Leonard Rose. Gould now feels permanently at home at 110 St. Clair Avenue West.

1962 "Let's Ban Applause" appears in *Musical America* in February. Gould writes "An Argument for Richard Strauss" for *High Fidelity*. On April 6 and 8, he performs Brahms's Piano Concerto No. 1 in D minor, Op. 15, with the New York Philharmonic conducted by Leonard Bernstein, who seemingly distances himself from Gould's interpretation of the piece, causing a critical uproar. Gould also finds time to make his first music documentary for CBC radio. The piece is called *Arnold Schoenberg: The Man Who Changed Music*. It premieres on August 8.

1963 Columbia Records releases Gould's Six Partitas by Bach. CBC televises *The Anatomy of Fugue,* which includes Gould's own terrifically whimsical composition titled "So You Want to Write a Fugue." On April 22 he delivers at the University of Cincinnati the Corbet Music lecture titled "Arnold Schoenberg — A Perspective." In July he gives the MacMillan Lectures at the University of Toronto.

April 10, 1964 Performs the last public concert of his career, in Los Angeles. In 1964 he also receives the degree of Doctor of Laws from the University of Toronto.

January 10, 1965 CBC Radio broadcasts *The Prospects of Recording,* which in April 1966 Gould adapts as an article for *High Fidelity*. BBC tapes *Conversations with Glenn Gould,* a four-part series recorded in Toronto with interviewer Humphrey Burton.

1966 Records Beethoven's Piano Concerto No. 5 in B major, Op. 73 (the *Emperor*), with Leopold Stokowski. In May, Gould is featured on the CBC television program *Duo* with Yehudi Menuhin.

March 29, 1967 CBC television features Gould in *To Every Man His Own Bach.* He releases a recording of music by Canadian composers István Anhalt, Jacques Hétu, and Oskar Morawetz in honour of Canada's Centennial. On December 28, the first of three radio documentaries, *The Idea of North,* is broadcast. The series is known as *The Solitude Trilogy.*

November 12, 1969 Creates and produces the radio documentary *The Latecomers,* the second in *The Solitude Trilogy.* On November 23, his article "Should We Dig Up the Rare Romantics ... No, They're Only a Fad," is published in the *New York Times.*

February 18, 1970 CBC TV features Gould on the program *The Well-Tempered Listener,* in discussion with Curtis Davis. Gould performs on piano, harpsichord, and organ.

August 5, 1970 CBC airs the television version of *The Idea of North,* produced and directed by Judith Pearlman.

December 9, 1970 CBC TV airs *Glenn Gould Plays Beethoven* — including the *Emperor Concerto* — with the Toronto Symphony, conducted by Karel Ancerl, in honour of the Beethoven Bicentenary.

February 2, 1971 Writes and produces radio documentary *Stokowski: A Portrait for Radio.* It is broadcast on the European Broadcasting Union (EBU) throughout Europe and by the CBC in Canada. He records works by Bach, Bizet, Byrd, Grieg, and Schoenberg for Columbia Records.

1972 Provides the soundtrack for the film *Slaughterhouse-Five,* directed by George Roy Hill.

January 1974 Appears in the CBC radio documentary *Casals: A Portrait for Radio.*

February 20, 1974 Appears on the CBC TV show *Musicamera* in "The Age of Ecstasy," the first of a four-part series called *Music in Our Time.*

November 19, 1974 Does a CBC radio documentary, *Arnold Schoenberg, the First Hundred Years: A Documentary Fantasy.* This same year he does a series of four television programs, *Chemins de la musique,* produced for the ORTF, France.

February 1975 Again appears on CBC TV's *Musicamera* in "The Flight from Order: 1910–1920," part of the *Music in Our Time* series.

July 26, 1975 Gould's mother Florence dies. He is depressed and his friends urge him to seek psychiatric help. He starts to display schizophrenic-type behaviour. It is not known whether it is caused by a serious mental health problem or the massive amounts of medications that he takes from several different doctors. The video *Radio as Music* is produced this year.

March 25, 1977 The third installment of *The Solitude Trilogy, The Quiet in the Land,* airs on CBC radio.

December 14, 1977 CBC TV *Musicamera* broadcasts *Music in Our Time* No. 4, "The Artist as Artisan, 1930–40."

1978 Gould's article "In Praise of Maestro Stokowski" appears in the May 14 issue of the *New York Times Magazine,* a recycling of material first published in the *Piano Quarterly* in two parts in the same year under the title "Stokowski in Six Scenes."

April 2 and 9, 1979 CBC broadcasts the two-part documentary *Richard Strauss: The Bourgeois Hero.*

September 27, 1979 John McGreevy's production of *Glenn Gould's Toronto* airs on CBC TV. The Clasart film *Glenn Gould Plays Bach: (1) A Question of Instruments,* directed by Bruno Monsaingeon, is released.

1980 CBS records releases a two-record set: *Glenn Gould Silver Jubilee.*

1981 Release of the Clasart film *Glenn Gould Plays Bach: (3) Goldberg Variations,* directed by Bruno Monsaingeon.

1982 Gould's second recording of *The Goldberg Variations* is released by CBS Records. Gould has himself taped in August as a conductor and directs a performance of the chamber version of Wagner's *Siegfried Idyll* with local Toronto musicians.

September 27, 1982 Gould suffers the first of several strokes.

October 4, 1982, 11:30 a.m. Gould succumbs to a series of strokes and passes away.

October 15, 1982 At St. Paul's Anglican Church in Toronto, an ecumenical memorial service (Anglican, Catholic, Jewish, and Salvation Army) is held with several thousand in attendance. Music is provided by leading Canadian musicians as a fitting tribute to Glenn Gould.

ACKNOWLEDGEMENTS

The Great Gould is the total of many other efforts supporting mine, and many kindnesses and insights, quibbles and corrections — too many to list. Advice and input came from Cat Flack and Patricia Hluchy, Gordon Lightfoot, John Rea, my brother Michael and his son Christopher, Alexina Louie and Bruno Monsaingeon, my editors at Dundurn Press, Robert Russ of Sony, Faye Perkins, Lynne Lafontaine, Ana Sani, Gordon Monahan, Friedemann Sallis, and Brian Levine of the Glenn Gould Foundation. There's John Beckwith, my professor in years gone by, Victor Feldbrill, Clarence Doolittle, Stephen Posen, Kevin Bazzana, Angus Carroll, and Erika Neher. The Shaperos — Kate, Eric, and son Josh — are the truest of the true Gould believers. Peter Mettler, the great documentary-maker, counselled me, as did many others not usually associated with Gould — video artist Mike Hoolboom, for one — who suggested new ways to go when the old ones seemed overtravelled. Fred Binkley reminded of the great days of the recording industry. Andy Wainwright reminded me of another name-changing musician of note — Bob Dylan.

A number of long-time Gould intimates are no longer with us. Some took time to answer questions. Ray Roberts is one. Others, many I've known over the years, remained silent. "They're simply tired of talking about Glenn Gould," said one of their friends. Yet I was never unaware of their presence, and possibly of their collective feeling that they'd already said what needed to be said and it was time to move on. Thanks to them, too, I've also tried to say what needs to be said.

IMAGE CREDITS

81	Photograph by Dan Weiner. Reproduced with the permission of the Glenn Gould Estate and CBS Records.
82	Photograph by Jock Carroll. Reproduced with the permission of the Glenn Gould Estate.
88	Reproduced with the permission of the Glenn Gould Estate and Sony Music.
90	Photograph by Jock Carroll. Reproduced with the permission of the Glenn Gould Estate.
94	© All Rights Reserved Don Hunstein (photographer) and Sony Music Inc.
97 top	LAC. © All Rights Reserved Don Hunstein (photographer) and Sony Music Inc. Reproduced with the permission of Sony Music Entertainment Inc., the Estate of Glenn Gould, and Glenn Gould Limited.
97 bottom	© All Rights Reserved Don Hunstein (photographer) and Sony Music Inc. Reproduced with the permission of Sony Music Entertainment Inc., the Estate of Glenn Gould, and Glenn Gould Limited.
99	© All Rights Reserved Don Hunstein (photographer) and Sony Music Inc. Reproduced with the permission of Sony Music Entertainment Inc., the Estate of Glenn Gould, and Glenn Gould Limited.
102	Reproduced with the permission of the Glenn Gould Estate.
103	© All Rights Reserved Don Hunstein (photographer) and Sony Music Inc. Reproduced with the permission of Sony Music Entertainment Inc., the Estate of Glenn Gould, and Glenn Gould Limited.
104	*Deseret News.* Reproduced with the permission of the Glenn Gould Estate.